The Whole Alphabet:
The Light And The Dark

The Whole Alphabet:
The Light And The Dark

Edited by
Katie Camacho,
Jennifer D. Corley,
Justin Hudnall

SO SAY WE ALL

Cover design by Chloe Stokes
Interior design by Olivia Hammerman

ISBN: 978-0-9979499-4-0

So Say We All (SSWA) is a San Diego-based 501c3 non-profit organization whose mission is to help people tell their stories, and tell them better, through providing education, publishing, and performance opportunities.

www.sosayweallonline.com

Contents

Acknowledgements ix

Foreword xi

Leon Dekelbaum
   A List of Names 1
Luke Dumas
   You Were Really Big 7
Brittany Henn
   Escaping Myself 14
Stephanie Westgate
   Canary—forty-eight days 21
   Untitled No. 2 24
   And there will be a happy ending 27
   Woman 32
   In response to National Coming Out Day 36
Henry Aronson
   Singkil 39
Joseph Fejeran
   Per Diem 47
Marcel Monroy
   days like lost dogs 54
   It will be for me and I will want It 55
   Cherry 57
   well worn 58
Frank DiPalermo
   Perverted and Possessed 59

Melia Lenkner

Two Girls on a Rainy Evening 69

Mickey Brent

Cookies At Lisa's 70

Paul Georgeades

Cold Turkey 79

Catherine Moscatt

The Girl with The Magenta Hair 68

Joel Castellaw

Two Are Better Than One 88

Tyler King

Gemini 97

Joyce Wisdom

Baby Orchid
Is A Lesbian 99

Kelly Bowen

Tiger. 102

Edward Elliott

Freshly Baked Bread 109

Jasz Kuyaté Cabrera

Them 115

Kelsey Schultz

Honey. 121

Mateo Perez Lara

Diatribe and Rose Thorns 131
Queer Novena to Lost Things and St. Anthony 133

Frank DiPalermo

The Night Everything Changed. 135

Joan McNamara

Sexy High Heels. 144

Bradley Dyer

Tony. 146

Raine Grayson

We Are All Becoming A Gamble—Remembering
Pulse & the Queer History of Mourning **150**

Y.L. Schmeltz

Hidden Presence **161**

JD Burke

The Bad Gay **165**

Contributors **173**

Acknowledgements

So Say We All gratefully acknowledges the financial support from the California Arts Council, California Humanities, the City of San Diego Commission for Arts and Culture, and the supporting members of So Say We All toward making this work possible. We would also like to thank the incredible staff of the historic Diversionary Theatre, the numerous gracious storytellers from So Say We All's community, the owners and staff of Babycakes, Lestat's Coffee House, and City of San Diego Councilmember Chris Ward.

If you are inspired by the stories within this work and would like to support So Say We All—or to learn more about our many other programs—please visit us at www.sosayweallonline.com.

—So Say We All

Foreword

When you sit down with a collection of people's personal stories, you sit down to a promise: Get to know these people. Get to know yourself. Get to know your world. This collection holds that promise, plus a bonus! You get to know your *queer* world, because all these stories are from queer people.

A part of my own story helps explain this book. I arrived in San Diego in 2013, a white cis gay slowly admitting to middle age. I come from South Carolina by way of eighteen years in San Francisco. In San Francisco, you can't throw homemade eco-glitter without hitting a writer, or a queer person or (jackpot!) a queer writer. South Carolina? Not as much.

When I said goodbye to San Francisco with all my close queers and my gloriously talented writing group, I wondered whether San Diego would be closer to SF or to SC on the queer/writer/queer-writer continuum.

I settled into the new landscape of surfers, tacos and beer. I found So Say We All, the serious storytelling and writing nonprofit with the cute name. It's a small shop with two staff, which sets up a uniquely supportive and powerful cycle for all its endeavors. In the storytelling shows, the cycle works like this: You are in the audience at one show, on stage the next, then coaching other writers/storytellers, then backstage producing. And then back in the audience. I fell right in. I did all those things. Now I'm on the board of directors to boot.

The program we call The Whole Alphabet started in 2017 as a partnership with local progressive minister Francisco Garcia, who wanted to do a community project with queer people. The intention, in part, was to address the damage done to queer people for generations by formal religion. Ostracism, incarceration, murder, you know the list. It was a bold move, and some local queer writers did not come along for the ride because of the religious association. But SSWA was eager to rekindle the queer writing workshops it had held in the past, and the advisory group of queer storytellers realized that healing and unlikely connections are part of what SSWA and storytelling is about, and the church's youth room had a big pink cross and a rainbow flag, so we went for it.

The events of The Whole Alphabet started with two writing salons, in the back yard of local queer cafe Babycakes (RIP Babycakes). We found an everybody-in cycle for the salons: a few stories told by queer SSWA storytellers, followed by an open writing session using a prompt, and then readings of a few of the fresh new pieces. It worked. People showed up. People wrote on phones, laptops, and pads of paper. People made new connections as people and as writers. The salons led to a storytelling show as the capstone event of the church partnership.

SSWA continued The Whole Alphabet program with queer writers from the San Diego salons and beyond. It all led to the book you are holding.

Right now in 2021, in the damaged and struggling not-so-United States, the value of a new book of stories from a marginalized group carries extra weight and potential. Back in college in the 1990s, bell hooks was a favorite cultural theorist of mine and my peers in the anthropology program. As a queer Black woman, since the 80s hooks has written about the white dominant culture that many white people only began to understand in 2020. She speaks clearly about how it works, and how to counteract it:

> Dominator culture has tried to keep us all afraid, to make us choose safety instead of risk, sameness instead of diversity. Moving through that fear, finding out what connects us, revelling in our differences; this is the process that brings us closer, that gives us a world of shared values, of meaningful community.[1]

This little book is one way to find that connection. Get to it! Get to know these people. Get to know yourself. Get to know your world.

—Hunter Gatewood, San Diego, February 2021

---

1 hooks, *Teaching Community: A Pedagogy of Hope*, 2002

Leon Dekelbaum

A List of Names

Her name is Sarah and she is my mother.
When I was about seven or eight, she told us that if any of her children were gay, she would disown us.

It twirled in my mind and it sat there. At the time, I hadn't even gone through puberty yet. I'm not even sure I was conscious of what I was. But it sat there, heavy and fat. A hate-filled statement that seemed out of character.

My mother is not a bible thumper, and she isn't a conservative—she's an east-coast Jew who usually votes Democrat. But in her mind, it was the idea of *the other*. There were the Jews she surrounded herself with, and then there were non-Jews who had "different values." Homosexuals were even further away. A different species we had no knowledge of outside of shows like *Three's Company* that turned homosexuality into a prancing minstrel show. Whatever lewd things homosexuals did, whatever god they worshipped, nothing like that was going to happen in *our family*.

Her name was Jen.
She was one of my best friends in high school. She came out as a lesbian when I was sixteen. I would test my mother by telling her about Jen. Jen has a new girlfriend. Jen is taking her to prom. My mother would shake her head and respond, "Her poor mother."

His name was Josh.

He was my other best friend. He loved musical theatre. In high school, his parents sat him down and told him that if he was gay, it would be ok with them. They loved him anyway. I was jealous of his wonderful parents. Josh wasn't gay.

His name was Nathan.

He was the first real homosexual I had ever talked to. I was nineteen and in college. I meet him in the International Perspectives on Gay and Lesbian History class that I had taken. I had no interest in International Perspectives on Gay and Lesbian History or the long discourses on whether Willa Cather was actually a lesbian or whether the term "history" should be "herstory." I simply wanted to get laid, and since this time predated Grindr, I had no idea how to meet guys.

Nathan and I were the only two gay men in the class besides the guy who wore a skirt every day and had pink hair. The rest were lesbians and open-minded "bi" guys with girlfriends.

Nathan and I had nothing in common. He seemed like a caricature to me. He was Wiccan. He had long spindly hands like two menacing spiders that crept and moved when he spoke. I thought he smelled vaguely of old semen. Nathan would go on about how oppressive and homophobic the University of Maryland was. How the previous day when he and his boyfriend thrust their hands down their pants in the dining hall, they were asked to stop. And when they refused, were told to leave.

I did not like Nathan, but he was a fascinating window into a world I never thought I would touch. After all, he had sex with a real boy and that small part of him made him almost a hero to me. I had never done as much as hold a guy's hand. I wondered, would I have to become like him to be gay? Would thrusting my hands down the pants of another boy in public seem ordinary and mundane?

His name was Antwon.
I met him at Sexual Minority Youth League in DC. I had been there several weeks, honestly just trying to meet someone. He had taken a liking to me and referred to me as "she." I had enough issues trying to awkwardly come out, I wasn't looking for anything that skirted gender. I informed him that I was very happy being a boy and if he harbored issues with his own gender identity, he would do best to leave me out of it. He reeked of baby powder and showed me his zippered thong telling me that he would make me his queen. I wondered if this would be my future?

His name was AJ.
When AJ showed up at the support group, we locked eyes across the room. The usual support group banter faded away. This one came home in a dress and his mother threw a shoe at him. This one wrote a 400-page poem about his one-night stand. I only saw AJ, and that's when I knew: we were going to devirginize each other.

That night he came over to watch a movie. We awkwardly sat there and I asked him- if he wanted a drink? AJ had never drank, so I offered him a shot out of the box of Alabama Slammers I kept in my fridge. I asked him if he wanted to smoke a bowl. AJ had never done that, so we smoked a bowl. And then we got each other off. AJ didn't feel right to me, but it was a start. A few months later I met Mark.

Mark was the first boy I ever loved.

I only wanted Mark. He wanted threesomes. He wanted pure intimacy some nights, and other times it was like someone built a wall in the middle of the bed. We took ecstasy together and stared at each other for hours. He finally broke up with me confessing that we were too much alike. I've spent the last fifteen years looking for that same problem.

Its name was Lambda Ki.

It was a gay frat in DC. Most of the members were a good twenty years out of college. I never had any interest in frats, but I joined, looking for brothers—gay brothers. I learned the Greek alphabet. I went through the motions. I wrote poems vowing I would never end up like them in bars by myself, and I quit after 5 weeks.

I missed being normal. I missed my family. I was pushing them away looking for a new one. But I couldn't tell them. So I lied to my mom when she asked if I was dating anyone. I lied when the Gay Society at Maryland sent a rainbow tassle to my house, when I specifically told them not to. I lied when the gay porn catalog was forwarded to their house over spring break. I invented all kinds of lies; I wove elaborate tales, big and small, complex and simple. I looked my mom in the eye and I lied freely. And I hated myself for it. But I didn't know how to stop.

His name was Damian.

He was #3 on the list I kept on the wall; my trophy of sexual conquests. We hooked up under the giant cross he had in his room. I was glad I was Jewish but I also knew that one night was all I needed with someone who had a giant crucifix in an otherwise barren room.

I don't remember the rest of their names. Some I met in bathhouses. Some in bars. Some at parties. There was one guy I knew as Cockroach who wore a possum skull around his neck. There was another one I blew in the Janitor's closet at the Magnetic Fields show. I kept the list to give value to what I was doing. I stopped at 100 because I ran out of room on the paper and I was ashamed. Putting this list on the wall made light of it. I could joke about it on the outside. *Look at me, I'm a gay slut.* On the inside, I felt dirty.

Her name was Luba.
I'd known her since Junior High. We were in college and she was one of my closest friends. She told me that she missed me. She never saw me anymore. I was avoiding her phone calls and never came to her dorm room. She wondered why I was pushing all my friends away. I told her about how everywhere I looked I just saw straight people: On TV. On campus. In my family. I just needed to fit somewhere. But I started to wonder if I really had to become another person.

I never learned his name.
I never talked to him. I was going to another gay bar by myself. I was in Philly for work. The bar was called Shampoo or Hairspray. He was standing outside under a streetlight. Waiting for someone, someone to pay him. He was crying. His tears reflected the light a little. I never went in. I knew that none of this was me. I didn't want to become like him. I was afraid I would. I wanted to find part of myself again.

I started composing my coming out letter to my mom on the way back to the hotel. It burst out of me that night. I went straight to my room and wrote for four hours in an insane, possessed way. I didn't need to edit or make a second draft. I wrote it all by hand. I refused to get up to pee or when my arm went numb from leaning on it. I just needed to say it and finish. I was worried if I moved I would lose it; I would never be able to start again. I needed her to understand, because I believed it would stop me from becoming somebody else.

My name is Leo and I am your son and I love you. But I'm tired of lying to you.
I started off by allaying what I thought would be her biggest fear. I was never going to become a Streisand impersonator. Then I told her that I will never change. I might as well change my eye color or decide to be left handed. I will never, ever, ever be with a woman. I will give you grandkids and most likely they will be brown, or yellow, or black, but you will love them because they will be your family. I read it all aloud to her. I went on and on. Finally I finished and waited.

She looked at me. Tears in her eyes. And with her voice quivering a little bit she said:

"Leo. You still need to date Jews."

Luke Dumas

You Were Really Big

I live a life of humiliation, but the most embarrassing, most shameful thing I ever did was get thin for a couple years.

You might imagine that being obese, as I am now, would be more embarrassing than having once been thin—and sure, daring to be a fat person in the world is a never-ending saga of degradation. Like earlier this year, when I was at an after-hours work event and a woman in her seventies, a complete stranger, made a beeline through the crowd toward me. Her eyes narrowed on my body, twinkling with savage purpose. Prepared always for public humiliation, I half suspected what was coming even before she laid a hand on my shoulder, bowed her head toward my ear, and said, "Now, I'm gonna offend you."

"Okay," I said.

"There's this program on Netflix, it's called *Walk for Life*," she said. (Not a real show, by the way—I checked.) "Now, I want you to watch this program and *really* watch it. Because if you don't change, you're gonna die."

As far as I'm concerned, that's a death threat.

And yet, I'd rather sit beside that woman on a long-haul flight, smashing my arms down over my stomach and sides so as not to encroach on her precious space as she quizzes me about what I ate for breakfast that morning, than run into an acquaintance I haven't seen since I gained the weight back. Sometimes I can't avoid it, and I imagine they look at me like one of those unemployed redneck families who win the lottery and blow it all on diamond-encrusted teeth and nickel slots. They look at me and think, *You stupid son of a bitch, you had it all and you threw it away. You had the world in the palm of your hand and you ATE IT!* I think of all the friends I made when I was thin and how disgusted they must be by the "new" me. In my head, every person I've ever dated spends hours every day trawling through my recent Facebook photos saying, "Wow, really dodged a bullet there!"

But I'm not a bullet.

I'm more of a cannonball if anything.

The truth is, other than those couple mortifying years, I've been fat my entire life and believed I always would be. Then at eighteen, I moved to Chicago for college, and while my classmates were all packing on the Freshman Fifteen, I was actually *losing* weight. Partly because I had to walk everywhere like an Eastern European peasant woman. Partly because I was eating all of my meals in a dining hall, which made it really hard to scarf down leftover Lo Mein standing in the harsh light of the open refrigerator at two o'clock in the morning. And partly because my college's core curriculum required everyone to take at least two P.E. classes, which was horseshit but also, I guess, kind of worked. By the time summer came, I'd lost thirty or forty pounds. Suddenly, for the first time in my life, normal weight wasn't actually that far out of reach. The thing that had always been my go-to shooting-star, blow-out-the-birthday-candles kind of wish felt, now, like a real possibility.

I went back to my then-home of Tucson, Arizona, determined to be normal weight. Every night that summer, I would finish my punishing gig as a camp counselor in charge of 25 six-year-old boys, then head to the gym for an hour or two of high-intensity cardio to a soundtrack of "Bad Romance" and "Womanizer." I did this five or six, sometimes seven nights a week. Holy shit, did the fat come off. The first week I lost eight pounds; the second week, nearly as much. Each successful weigh-in spurring me on to keep going, push harder, embrace the hunger. I rolled up to college that fall at my all-time lowest weight of 155 pounds and people were like, "Who the fuck is *that?*" I got compliments I'd never received in my life. Or maybe I had but they felt different now. "You look great!" people would say, and suddenly my first thought wasn't, *No, actually I'm an enormous fat pig.*

Who knows? Maybe someone would even date me.

Of course, I was nineteen and had zero confidence, so walking into a Boystown gay bar and trying to pick up some random daddy was not going to work for me. Inevitably—and by that I mean, as my first and only step—I turned to the heady pages of Gay.com. I cobbled together a profile of lies and flattering photos, and spent hours searching for my First Great Love. Of course I was too insecure to actually contact anyone on the site, even though there were plenty I liked the look of. But it didn't matter, because within a couple of days I had received my first message.

Hi there, it read. *You're really cute. Want to grab coffee sometime?*

It was the first time anyone had even acknowledged me in a more-than-platonic way. I couldn't believe it. My first date, sure to be my first boyfriend—probably even the love of my life.

Then I looked at his profile.

The message was from a guy named Daniel, a Colombian grad student at the Business School. At thirty-one, he was older, but I didn't mind that so much. It was the photo that was the bigger concern. Let's just say, there wasn't an immediate attraction. Imagine a pug with a large, mushroom-shaped nose and bushy black eyebrows like Martin Scorsese and you may be in the vicinity.

Look, "ugly" is a strong word—a mean, hateful word, like the way some people use "fat," and as soon as it entered my mind I felt awful. After all, if his profile was anything to go by, Daniel seemed perfectly nice. He liked pizza and traveling and going to the movies, which were all great things to like. Out of the thousand Chicago-area men on Gay.com, he chose me to send a message to—*me!* I imagined being on his side of the computer screen: putting myself out there to someone and not even getting a response back. Hearing, in their silence, that cruel, hateful word echoing back at me again and again and again.

Hey Daniel, I wrote. *Thanks for your message. I'd love to get coffee sometime. When are you free?*

We agreed to meet at the Business School food court. The place was vast, thronging, and unfamiliar to me. He wasn't there when I arrived, so I grabbed a drink and waited at a table. Finally he appeared in the crowd, and my secret hope that it had just been a really bad picture was obliterated.

"Luke?" He held out a hand, business-like. I matched his firm grip. He wore rectangular glasses and a chunky sweater over a button-down shirt. He looked like the kind, understanding father figure in a Disney movie about children who fall into an ancient, leather-bound book and go on an adventure with a goblin who looks mean but is just misunderstood. "Sorry I'm late," he said, in his perfect English. "Oh—you already got a drink." So he went to grab a coffee as I held the table, kicking myself and thinking, *Why am I here?* He was old and kind of stuffy and I didn't find him attractive at all. The thought of kissing him made my head instinctively rock backwards on my neck. Of course I wasn't going to just get up and leave, but I decided before he'd even returned to the table that this would be the last time I saw him.

That night, Daniel sent me a message letting me know how much he had enjoyed our date, that there was a movie playing on the northside he wanted to take me to and a good tapas place nearby. I was aware, even then, that simply ignoring the invitation was an option—but it just didn't feel right.

Hi Daniel, I wrote. *It was really nice meeting you today. I think you're a great guy but I'd like to just be friends. I thought the age difference wouldn't matter to me, but unfortunately it does. I'm so sorry.*

He responded almost immediately.

No problem. Let's be friends. Are you free for dinner and a movie on Friday night?

Jesus, Daniel, I thought, can't you take a fucking hint? Yet having told him I wanted to be friends, I couldn't then refuse to hang out with him—could I?

I agreed to the movie—one final concession to politeness. I hoped.

It was probably about twenty degrees that night, the wind searing and powerful. So strong, I could actually feel it knock me back as I stood waiting for Daniel on the platform of the 59th Street Metra station. So strong, it threatened to blow me off my feet.

Wind could do that now. I couldn't help but smile at the thought.

Daniel arrived and immediately went in for the hug. His spicy cologne hit me like a palmful of black pepper and tobacco being smashed into my face.

"You look great," he said, looking me up and down, and that's when I realized that I had been had. It was a second date all right, and given my track record of not being able to say no, it probably wouldn't even be the last. I had a vision of myself trapped in an endless loop of dates and charming follow-up messages, month after month, year after year, until finally he was kneeling before me in a crowded restaurant sliding a ring on my finger and I was thinking, *Fine—but just for a year or two, I mean it!*

Then, as we stood waiting for the northbound train, Daniel said something that changed everything.

"So," he said, "I was looking at your old Facebook photos.... You were really big, weren't you?"

I shot him a look out of the corner of my eye, daring him to go on. "Mm hmmmm."

He said, "You must have eaten *a lot*."

A wild flurry of emotion surged through me, attended by a couple of pressing questions. First, how does a person who looks like the floating eyeball monster in *Big Trouble in Little China* have the balls to comment on my appearance, past or present? Second, who exactly—and I mean this literally—who exactly did he think he was talking to?

You must have eaten a lot. As if he didn't realize the "you" in that scenario was the same "me" that was standing on the platform, glaring at him with bitter contempt. As if he had gone onto Facebook and happened upon a picture of some sort of alternate-dimension me, an abstract idea of what I could have been rather than the person I actually (still) was. Sure, maybe the guy was just making small talk. Maybe in some messed-up way he actually thought he was flattering me. Did he really think that because I'd lost some weight, I would be cool with his open disgust for my body and the mindless gluttony he was so quick to project onto it?

That's what the weight-loss commercials and diet gurus don't tell you about getting thin: your entire life up until that point becomes nothing more than a "before." You're reminded daily that, no matter how smart or accomplished or kind you were when you were fat, you only really started to count as a human being once you got thin.

Even now that I'm fat again, people still want to treat my body as if it were somehow apart from me—like a flu or something. A problem that, once solved, disappears forever and without a trace. They don't understand that my fatness isn't just the weight I carry on my body—it's way more than that, it's the weight I carry in my mind. They don't get that even at my thinnest, I would look in the mirror and see the same unattractive, overweight body staring back at me, every ounce of remaining flab magnified in my mind's eye to match my enduring self-loathing. They don't get that I don't need some creep to tell me how worthless I was and am—there's already one in my head, who never lets me forget.

At the end of the night, we rode the number six bus back to the southside. As we were nearing his stop Daniel said, "Want to come back to my place for a drink?"

This time, I didn't pad the rejection with a gentle lie about having to get some reading done or waking up early the next morning.

I looked over at him with an air of considered appraisal, and said, "No thanks."

Brittany Henn

Escaping Myself

Growing up, I always had a feeling I was gay. Or something. As early as age six, I would explore the internet on my Nana's computer where I found Moshi Monsters, Club Penguin—and soft lesbian porn. Back then, YouTube didn't have a lot of the guidelines it has today for videos and it was easy to access a lot of R-rated content.

One day when the whole family was sitting eating Church's Chicken, my Nana just straight out asked "Now, who was watching 'Hot Sexy Girls Making Out' on the computer?!"

I hesitated. "Not me," I said and continued to eat my mashed potatoes. From that day forward, though, I made sure to delete my browser history.

I also have two cousins, one of whom is a lesbian and the other a trans woman. This introduced the idea that loving or being attracted to someone of the same sex was possible. On the other hand, my mom was a pastor's kid and we went to church pretty often. Sometimes I would even sleep under the benches during three-hour services, waiting for free food when it was over. I didn't get the sense that homosexuality was wrong religiously until I was a bit older. That's when I overheard my family speaking about my queer cousins in a more negative way. I realized everyone only tolerated them, rather than accepted them, for who they are.

I was about eight when I discovered anti-LGBT propaganda, a lot of it based on religion. Still, I was conflicted. I didn't know that people like my family lived in other states, and queer people are still fighting for their rights there as well. They are still being discriminated against, they are still being killed for loving someone, and they are still dying for believing in something greater. I'd see pictures of the Westboro Baptist Church signs online that read "God Hates Gays," and would think, "God can't hate me, I go to church and pray."

Still, I knew I was attracted to women, even then. It would take years for me to fully understand my own sexualtiy.

My life would've been different, maybe even easier, if my dad hadn't passed away when I was four. When he passed, it awoke the start of my clinical depression and it was hard for me to express my emotions. Once I started elementary school, I was bullied and had to change schools twice. I was a shy, vulnerable, chubby, and an overall annoying *High School Musical* fan who didn't know how to shut up. The combination of losing my father, being rejected by my peers, trying to suppress my interest in girls, and being put on various medications took a huge toll on my mental health at such a young age. On top of all that, my mom remarried when I was seven and my new stepfather and I did not get along. This was something that eventually changed, but was difficult at first. I was most happy when I wasn't home.

I was twelve when I started middle school, which was one of the happiest times in my life. I was surrounded by friends and had amazing adventures with them, and this was also when I learned more about my sexuality. A lot of my friends were very fluid and open about their sexualities, and it was a nice feeling being around people who understood me. My first year of middle school I came out as bisexual. The words just came out one day as I was sitting on the blacktop with my friends after PE class. They weren't fazed and said, "Oh, we kind of already knew."

I tried to embrace and be proud of my sexuality. I used to have a gaming Instagram account that got pretty popular at the time, and I put my sexuality in my bio. Unfortunately, since I didn't have a phone of my own, I would use my mom's. One day I forgot to log out.

She confronted me. "What is this? Why do you have that there?" I told her to leave me alone, because I wasn't ready to tell her anything. I knew religion was a big thing for her, and I didn't want to be lectured. She called my Aunt Patty, my dad's eldest sister. After my mom was done, my aunt wanted to talk to me, but I didn't want to tell her anything either. At one point, she said, "It is just a phase," which looking at it now, was true. Being bisexual was a *huge* phase for me. It was the first step in a journey towards understanding every aspect of my sexuality and identity.

After middle school came high school, also known as hell. As a plus-size teen struggling with both body image and identity, it weighed heavily on me. I always wore baggy clothes to hide not only my size, but my femininity. I just felt miserable with my body and myself. I was away from all my friends and everyone I loved. I was alone and an outcast all over again. I started skipping class, hiding in the restrooms to cry or harm myself. I attempted suicide more times than I remember in the first three years of high school, beginning in my freshman year. By then, I was learning more about my sexuality. I knew by the end of my freshman year that I was transgender, but

I had no one to talk about it with. I felt helpless. So I hid. I began to dress in oversized men's clothes. I hated my breasts and being associated with females; I hated being seen as a girl. This is where I first adopted the name Nate. I was so in love with Nathan Drake from a video game called *Uncharted* that I wanted to claim that name as my own.

I moved schools again for my sophomore year. This would be a fresh start that I needed. I was more open to my teachers about my identity and asked them to address me as Nate, even though I said nothing about this to my mother or stepfather. I gave myself a faux mohawk cut and I felt okay. The self harm and suicidal thoughts didn't end, though. I still didn't have many friends that I felt comfortable talking to. The walk between my home and school involved walking on a highway overpass. So many times, I thought about jumping. The only thing that helped me overcome the urge was thinking about my family and my little siblings. The image of seeing them cry over me being gone still breaks me now. I never wanted to break their hearts. I just wanted my pain to go away.

I was still struggling to find others who thought like me, when one of my friends from middle school asked if I wanted to go to San Diego Pride with them. I was really excited and wanted to experience it for myself, but how was I going to ask my mom? Until then, I'd only talked about my identity openly with my friends and teachers. Then I realized that this was my best chance to tell my mother. She would see how badly I wanted to go to Pride. I remember crying to my step dad first, telling him how trapped I felt, and how I really wanted to attend San Diego Pride that year. He surprised me by saying, "It's really up to your mother; none of this is going to change what I think of you, because you are still you."

I remember standing in a small hallway of our old apartment hugging him and crying into his shirt.

The next couple of days passed. I still hesitated to ask my mom. I was terrified of what she might say, I was afraid she would say no and not accept me for who I was. Finally, she confronted me. "What's the matter?" she asked. Her face was scared and concerned. I started to cry. Then she held me tight while I sobbed into her shirt. We then sat down on her bed, facing one another, I just spoke with my heart.

"I know you probably don't want to hear this, but it is hurting me inside to be keeping this in. I hate being a woman, I want to be a man. I don't feel comfortable with my body, I feel disgusting!"

She didn't say anything, just looked at me as I looked down at her black and gold comforter. "You know I will always love you," she said. "This isn't right, but I will love you regardless." When I asked if I could go to Pride with my friends, she thought about it for a second. "Letting you go would be like feeding you to the wolves."

My heart kind of broke. A part of me knew why she didn't want me to go. I was young and maybe she didn't want to be seen as a bad parent. Still, I needed to see what was out there for myself. I walked out of the house on that Friday evening so I could stay that night with my friend. I didn't have money for a bus, let alone know which one to take, so I walked from our apartment complex in Chula Vista to my friend's house in Imperial Beach, a six-mile walk, all on my own. I was driven by the freedom and the determination to go to San Diego Pride the next day.

Using public transit for the first time was awful. My friend and I were both clueless and worried. Luckily, we spotted some fellow queers who were dressed up for the occasion on the trolley and followed their lead. When we got off the number seven bus right on University Avenue, in Hillcrest, the heart of San Diego's LGBT+ community, I felt alive and without worry. As we walked toward the parade, I felt so free and energized. The rain poured. The streets flooded. My worn-down shoes filled up with water. None of it bothered me, because I was so excited to see other people like me. I saw people of every size, color, religion, identity, everyone! I had fallen in love with a community I didn't know existed here in my home of San Diego. Even though it was pouring rain, the show still went on; everyone was still having the time of their lives, smiling and spreading the love.

The experience of being around people like me helped give me new meaning in life. In my junior year, I transferred schools again, but this time I was where all my friends were. I joined the Gay-Straight Alliance and later became club president my senior year. Being a part of the club also helped me decide what I wanted to do after high school. I loved creating safe spaces for LGBT+ youth, and being surrounded by like-minded people. Being able to work with amazing teachers and organizations like Gay, Lesbian, and Straight Education Network (GLSEN) San Diego, The Trevor Project, and so many more helped me resist self-harming and suicidal thoughts. I worked at the local library and started my own Gay-Straight Alliance for youth outside of school, one of the best decisions I've ever made. As my life changed for the positive, my relationship with my parents improved. I used to believe they had to accept the situation as soon as I told them my identity and sexuality. I grew angry at them because they didn't want me to be proud of my identity at the time. I also was angry with myself, by not being patient and understanding that they needed time to process the situation. I learned later that it takes time for someone to understand the new you. Even now, it is still a process with them, but they are proud of me for how devoted I am to the LGBT+ community and my passion for equal rights.

I continue to understand more about my sexuality, my identity, and I no longer identify as trans. I am non-binary. I feel more comfortable with androgyny. I want someone to look at me one day, wonder if I am male or female, but then give up and see me as a person. I still go by Nate, and more recently have taken up the name Pixel as a nickname and online alias that is more neutral. Still, most of my friends all know me as Nate. My family still calls me by my birth name, which I have accepted even if I no longer would accept that from my friends. I do not consider myself bisexual anymore, I am queer. I love that term so much because it's neutral and it just means my sexuality is very fluid even though I am more attracted to women.

Now I am nineteen, living in Arkansas, and still striving to pursue my activism. It is a close-minded state, but I am always ready for a fight. I have escaped a part of me that was holding me back from change and seeing a future for myself, and I am so glad I did. I will always fight depression and suicidal thoughts, but I will always find a reason to look forward to the future. People all over the world and throughout our country are being discriminated against, being killed for loving someone, and still dying for believing in something greater. I have found joy in fighting for equality, and not only for LGBT+ rights. I will fight for women's rights, black rights, latinx rights, and the rights of all minorities facing backlash from mainstream society. I want to educate people and be an ally to those who need them most. I want to protect LGBT+ youth suffering from mental illness and let them know that they can keep going. It may be slow, but things do get better.

Stephanie Westgate

Canary—forty-eight days

I googled my old name, and the only
story featured was a man with my
old name was killed in prison forty-eight
days after pleading guilty
to raping an eleven-year-old girl.

We were the same age.

He died days after I came out, and I don't
know if Google is showing truth

or is a canary for my future—
my neighbors kid saw me in a dress:

it was night, and I thought
I had waited long enough, checked
mirrors and over my shoulder enough

to make sure no one
could see me like this, but

he was in my blind spot, and the next day
his father was at my gate with arms long

and clenched, his face
mixed with inconvenience and *how dare you*

and fear.

I've learned to live between held breaths
to notice the difference between the main
door and stall doors closing

and to count
to carry hand sanitizer and never
wash hands in public or else

I contaminate the clean

I extend the stares, and huffs from people
protecting sheltered young eyes
from becoming my victims

and I'm scared my old name being killed
is the canary finalizing

I'm a crime.

But, maybe it won't be so bad, maybe
I'll be one of those punk rock criminals

Maybe I'll be fantasized about
be taught in lectures

maybe I'll have fans, men
and women alike sending letters begging
to be with me

maybe I'll be folk heroed, be sung—
I'll go out in a hail of bullets, but remembered
for fighting off the world—

or, maybe, if only the good die young,
I'll retirement home, grow old

next to my husband or wife
we'll have kids, they'll still
visit every Sunday for tea

or maybe we'll just run
from forest to beach stopping only
to carve our names in tree
and watch the sunset...

maybe

Stephanie Westgate

Untitled No. 2

A man followed   me
                onto the trolley:

the entire ride widening
        his eyes to me
            drinking   /   echoing
Hey girl
                Hey GIRL   hey girl   hey GIRL
                    HEY GIRL
                    HEY GIRL
I didn't want
                to exit on
my stop for fear   he'd follow
        me home   but
        I also
    didn't want to exit before

for fear he'd follow me and
                    I'd have no
way to get home
                so I ran
        exited

                    my stop and ran and
                                        as I left
he glued his face
            to the window and drooled.

I didn't stop until I was safely
                    behind double
                    locked doors and panting
                                                    I'm safe.

                    He didn't do anything.
I'm safe.
                    before calming /

thinking   at least he thought I was a girl.

I have an abusive relationship with being seen.

I look in the mirror and see a jigsaw
                                        puzzle forced
            together in a way supposed
                    to be artsy   but really's
just broken   and wrong—

            my face's too long and furry
            shoulders too broad
            fingers too sausage
            my dick…   is there—

the only
     reason I'm so out
       about my identity is
I feel there's no way   I could

actually be seen as my true self, so
          I might as well
get in front and buffer
        the hate   even if
this conclusion of myself is

          regularly
               proven false:
I texted a friend that night
(through tears)   and she

said ever since she met
     me, she's only seen me   as a wonderful woman.

I don't know why I put more stake in strange men trying
to fuck me   than friends   who actually love me

     I don't know why I'm always waiting for the worst.

Yesterday, I   put on makeup and
          a bow in my hair
and actually felt cute   like really cute.

I went to work like that.
Looked in a mirror

          nothing broke.

Stephanie Westgate

And there will be a happy ending

It is now and she says she wanted
to look cute for me because last time I
looked cute for her, and this

is the end of the scene.
It is also the beginning
—it is everything—

and all I have the capacity to do is
       [awkward movements and solitary pacing,
       moving hands from held behind
       my back, keeping my spine from melting
       with happiness, to over my heart, to
       a suffocation pillow for my smile
       because it's gotta look really dumb and toothy
       and I don't want her to see me dumb and toothy
       because what does this mean
       does this mean she also   feels this?]

It is now, and I'm on a hotel bed
in a city full of people who know
way too much about the person I'm supposed to be

and I'm letting my mom in
on my best kept secret

and she is tired
just wants me to stop
talking so she can sleep, now keeping
me up with the question / accusation

but you don't like men

and this is the beginning of the scene
the beginning of marrying who
I am with
who I love

and it is now, and I'm actually
contemplating getting off
the trolley with him

I've repeated

to him I have a dick
that I'm not real and he doesn't want me

but he repeats yes
he does
I'm pretty
this is his stop
let's go have fun

but it doesn't feel full like that
because it is now and she's

showing me pictures of clothes she tried on
and I'm showing her pictures of clothes I tried on
and we're complementing each other

saying damn
and yass
and it feels full like that
I feel full like that

and we're both smiling

and it is now and I'm not smiling
I'm on the hotel bed listing every
guy friend's name I can think of trying

to convince my mom I once
liked them more

and she's not buying it
and I'm not buying it

and it is now and I'm trying
to convince a friend I have a crush
on a guy in our class
and she's not buying it

and I'm forcing myself to buy it more
this comes after I wore a dress seriously

for the first time
after I promise myself when
I do this girl thing full time I will

be a good one
I'll only wear dresses
and heels

I'll have a boyfriend
and love him like a good girl should

and it is now and I haven't been a good girl
I'm watching him leave the trolley
I'm punishing myself for letting
him leave because the good girl would have gone with

the good girl would have smiled
and gone with and did as he said

I'm cursing my work uniform for mandating pants
cursing myself for not shaving my legs
and being okay with pants so he couldn't
see what a bad girl I am

But it is now, and she's complimenting me
saying damn and yass to photos, none
of which are of me in a dress

and still, I feel good

It is now, and I know I'm good
I know I'm good

It is now, and I haven't seen her
in over three months, our texts
are usually short and repetitive
and I don't know what this means

and I don't want to know what this means
like, she's busy
I'm busy
it doesn't have to mean more than that
I don't want to know if it means more than that

but, like
if it does
would that really change anything?

It is now, early morning and I'm walking to work
and she's probably getting off work
and I'm walking watching the sun
rise bright and gold

and like, damn

so that's how it feels to be seen

Stephanie Westgate

Woman
**in response to *Menstruation*
by Anita D**

For the first time
I'm happy
while in therapy

I'm happy, and telling
my therapist I heard rumors
that some people
experience period-like symptoms
while on hormones

I'm happy
because there's a chance
I could be closer
to complete woman.

This realization comes after
my aunt yelled me out
of the restaurants bathroom

after she said I don't
have her parts
have womans parts so I don't belong
in a woman's space

after friends reminded me
I can't have a period
or give birth
or feel the pain of woman

the pain and fear
being woman is not something
I can just jump into—I did
not grow up as one so I can not
now call myself one

But I'm happy
because this
might finally be
my ticket into this club.

My therapist smiles.
Says *good for you.*
Says *when you gonna start?*

Meaning when you gonna start hormones.
Meaning when you gonna start actively
                    trying to be a woman.

Not meaning start realizing you already are one
start realizing the body
doesn't make the person.

I'm always asked *but how*
do you know, like really

know?

I always say because I just do.
Because I woke up this morning.

Because there was this neighborhood girl
that thought it was so funny
when she did my nails and makeup

like, it became her thing to do
when the younger kids and us
older kids got together, and after

I'd leave it on
for as long as possible, wearing also
my most natural smile

to the point where I
was the one trying to convince her
to make me look pretty

and yes, I know makeup
and painted nails don't make woman

just like I know periods and pregnancies
don't make woman, for the qualities

of woman can't
be checked off a list

Woman is not this or that
Woman just is.

I am woman.
I am woman.
I am woman.
I am woman. I know

because I'm happy

Stephanie Westgate

In response to National Coming Out Day

The person
to which I am talking

refers
to me
and my identity/transition
as that time
I "became Stephanie."

As in this is something new.
As in I am not who I was.
As in I'm now worse/worse off, and while I know

this is not true
that I am who I always
was, just now more owning it,

it is hard
because at times

I wish it was.

I wish "coming out" mandraked

me into some new person:
someone whose body validated
their identity and femininity

without trauma or question.

The next person
to which I am talking also invalidates

me with the statement *if*

gender norms didn't exist, if
men could freely wear dresses, I
would just be a man and not this
frankensteined concoction of a woman, and while

I know this is not true
I know my gender/identity goes much
deeper than what is put on my body

that it is my body
it is hard
because at times I wish
it was just that simple.

I am prone to running away.
I do not like conflict or change, and now
my life is nothing but.

But I also know running
away is how lies become
normalized and facted.

I am learning the value of directions.

I know
I will probably never
feel fully comfortable in my body
and will always be scared and running, but

it's where I run that matters.
It's to what I'm running that matters.

It's making sure
I gain enough speed, that all
barriers dam open

with flooded change to tide
strength to those just taking their first steps.

Henry Aronson

Singkil

Like every other Filipino kid, I had a nickname: Biboy. Not for my non-existent breakdancing skills. I wasn't the male equivalent of the b-girls of New York Subways. I'm named after my dad—the first Biboy. My pops was mestizo, a mixed-blood Filipino. His father, my grandfather, was a Russian Jew, hence the last name Aaronson. My Lola was the granddaughter of a Spanish Friar and a local girl. Colonialism. You figure it out. Another vestige of colonialism is the way Filipinos adopted the nickname "boy." At the turn of the century, American soldiers fought in the Philippines during the Spanish American War and then the failed Philippine revolution. Those GIs, steeped in the racism prevalent at the time, called the brown skinned Filipino men "boys." Instead of taking the epithet as an insult, Filipinos adopted it as a nickname. There's a boy in every Pinoy family: Jim-Boy, Jo-Boy, Roy-boy, Am-boy, or plain old Boy.

Dad's nickname was Big Boy, but eventually became Biboy because too many of his peers and family kept dropping the "-ig." I inherited his nickname. Before I realized my father's name wasn't Dad, I thought my name was more of a command, a mandate; as in, "Be good." "Be-have!" "Be boy!" I suspected my nickname reflected my parents' ambivalence for a gay son. That's not how I phrased it back then. They knew my secret—that I wasn't a real boy. Real boys like girls, and I liked boys. I liked men. In kindergarten, I wanted to see what it would feel like to be naked with my classmate Drew Lawrence. I got all tickly and prickly inside when I saw our principal, this bear of a man, strip naked in the swimming pool dressing room. He was so hairy and strong. I had this huge crush on my fifth grade teacher, Mr. Cima. I couldn't keep my eyes off the stray hairs that poked out from underneath his button down shirts or through the sleeves of his t-shirt when we were in PE. I knew without having to be told directly that there was something wrong with this kind of longing, but didn't realize the word for my desire until much later in life. I knew I was not the right kind of boy.

To complicate matters, I wasn't even considered a boy in my family. There was me, my sister Princess, and my two brothers, who everyone called the boys. I wasn't one of the boys. I was someone or something that needed to be reminded, ordered to "Be boy." The boys were rough and tumble guys. They played football, baseball. They boxed. I boxed, too. Actually, I got boxed by the boys, even though they were three and five years younger than me. Dad boxed me, too. Years later, Princess told me that he beat me a lot more than the couple times I can consciously remember. She believed that at first, dad was trying to rough me up, to make me tough. But she saw that the boxing became more and more about dad's anger. The one time I remember him beating me royally was when I got my report card in fourth grade. I got good grades. Great grades. But I got a "U"—unsatisfactory—in citizenship for talking too much in class. Dad slapped me when he read the report card. I was shocked, because I had good grades. Who cares about citizenship grades? He said it's because I talk too much; like a girl. Disgust in his eyes.

I don't know where the chutzpah came from, but I answered, "Talking a lot doesn't make me a girl," lilting in a tone that probably confirmed my sissy status. He punched me in the gut. I rolled over—ducking and covering like they taught us—and he proceeded to slap, kick, and shove me from one room to the other. We made the entire circuit of the house: living room through the hallway, past the bathroom, to the kitchen, through the dining room and back to the living room. He whaled on me. Hard.

So for obvious reasons, I avoided coming out to my parents for as long as I could. In fact, I didn't come out as much as was pulled out.

Mom summoned me into the kitchen. This was it. The kitchen was *the* room for serious discussions. Grades. Groundings. This was the night I announced to everyone that I broke up with my girlfriend of one year, Laura. I never meant to be with a woman. When I met her, I had already decided I'd need to come out. But Laura pursued me, sending me flowers anonymously and leaving me love notes. The notes never mentioned her sex, so I was all thrilled to be courted. When she revealed herself, I immediately told her I was gay and I hadn't thought I'd ever be with a woman. We went out with a couple of friends to a club, got drunk, she made moves, and I succumbed. The sex was good. I did have feelings for her, and I tried to convince myself that perhaps I was bisexual. Plus, being chased felt like an aphrodisiac—and like so many other scared, closeted gay men, I harbored the hope that me and Laura would work out. But the relationship was doomed.

So the Sunday after we ended our relationship, the family sat around the living room, Mom on the couch crocheting, Dad in his recliner reading the editorials. My siblings and I were sprawled around the living room floor, sort of watching TV, sort of talking with each other. I matter of factly announced that me and Laura had broken up. Princess pursed her lips, side-eyed the boys. All three of them snuck out the room, covered by Mom audibly gasping and Dad snapping his newspaper and lowering his recliner, signaling his desire to avoid any further conversation. But not Mom. She wanted to talk.

Mom drew herself up, chin up, shoulders back, turned from the living room and, on the balls of her feet, glided toward the kitchen. She became the Moro princess dancing Singkil, her feet darting between clap, clap, clapping bamboo poles. In the Muslim-inflected traditional dance of the Philippines, the crisscrossing singkil poles represent falling trees and branches buffeted by a cataclysmic typhoon and earthquake. The clacking of the bamboo echoing exploding branches, booming thunder, and the cleaving of the earth. Ankles festooned with bells, the Muslim princess races against the natural disaster, accompanied by her faithful umbrella girl who follows her step for step as they avoid the sharp cracks of bamboo poles. Their bare feet slip in and out and between the clashing poles, shins and thighs feinting, jumping, testing, twisting and twirling across the poles. The princess' and umbrella girl's torsos remain frozen yet graceful in perfect posture, long balletic necks emerging from strong shoulders, eyes cast downwards over high cheekbones and upthrust chins.

Mom led me, her reluctant umbrella girl, to the dining table.

"I want to ask you something," she spoke in a broken whisper, but her question boomed in my ears like a blast from a typhoon.

"Sure, if you really want to know the truth," I muttered under my breath more to myself than to her. I read somewhere that kids will ask questions when they are ready to hear the answers to complex questions. Questions like, "Where did I come from?" "What is sex?" and other questions I never posed to my parents. Perhaps Mom was ready, but I certainly hadn't rehearsed for this ersatz singkil performance.

"What?" She apparently heard me above the imaginary bamboos her tsinela-clad feet dodged.

"Um, if you're ready for an answer, go ahead and ask," I could barely hear my voice above the rapidly increasing pounding of my heart, recalling the quickening pace of the singkil. She sat across from me, her orchids framing her. Her eyes remained thin. I saw the glimmer of tears. "You mean, you are gay?"

I coughed an affirmative sound and said "Yes, I am."

Tears streamed from her eyes, but she refused to dab her face, letting the tears track down her face. "Is it, is it, something I did? Is it something Daddy or I did?" she whispered tentatively, with greater fear than what I thought would be the harder question.

"No, Ma, it was nothing you or Dad did. It's not anything you did. It's just me." That's all I had.

"Then you are saying it was you? Not us?" She perked up a little. "Oh, I knew it. I knew it."

I nodded. I was thrilled to hear this—my mom understands. She understands me. She was always on my side! I knew it! She had always supported me in all my less than macho activities—when Dad cheered the boys on at PAL baseball and football leagues, Mom would sew costumes for my drama and dance productions. She'd run lines with me and rehearse my lines. When I was in *Oklahoma*, she was my Ado Annie to my Will Parker. She was my Polly to my Tony when I did *The Boyfriend*. I was her cavalier gentleman caller, escorting her to musicals that Dad didn't want to see. Together, we marveled at Liza Minnelli in *Cabaret* (didn't get the gay theme at all, but something in me definitely quivered), Barbra Streisand in *Funny Girl* and *Funny Lady,* and watched reruns of *Wizard of Oz* faithfully many years after the rest of the family got sick of us singing along with Judy Garland. Yes. My mom knew all along, I realized at that moment. Why was I afraid to let her know? She all but squired me into the world of musical theater!

Oh, and she's crying, too. She really feels for me! She's really on my side!

"Now I understand"—she continued more strongly—"understand," as her voice reached a fever pitch, "why you are such a bitch!"

I don't recall the rest of that conversation. My mind raced back and forth between being shocked and angry. It wasn't enough that she outed me, depriving me of my moment, my chance to be the Moro princess. I realized I disappointed her—more than I ever had imagined. I lost my protector, the one who would make it alright when I finally had the nerve to come out to my father.

My next vivid memory of that night was vainly trying to reread Tolkien's *Return of the King.* I had called friends in case I needed to make an escape. I was afraid my dad would beat me royally, like he'd done before. Easy to imagine.

While the hosts of Mordor battled the horse-people of Rohan at Minas Tirith, I could hear my mom caterwauling through the walls of our house. After I saw *Farewell My Concubine,* I realized what Mom sounded like: a cross between a nun chanting her rosary and the tragic warbling Chinese opera diva. Dad's rumbling voice punctuated my mother's arias every few minutes, his basso profundo contrasting her contralto wailing. I couldn't hear the exact words, separated as we were by a wall, but the tone did not console me. Was Dad comforting Mom? Or was she trying to calm him down?

Or were they egging each other on, preparing to come out the room and exile me right there? I feared the worst—expecting at every turn of the page to be buffeted by the kinds of blows Dad used to whale on me when I was younger.

After Samwise freed Frodo from the Orcs, but just before they met up with Gollum for the last time, I felt safe enough to bed down. I slept on the living room floor near the hall-way—the middle of the room was full of luggage and baby gear for my sister who had brought her first born Johnny to the house, and everyone else got dibs on a bed. When the boys and I shared a room, we only had two beds, so whoever forgot to call a bed got to sleep on the floor. So sleeping on the floor wasn't out of the ordinary—no cause for concern.

My parents had an early engagement the next day, and I awoke to hearing them walking from their bedroom at the end of the hallway to the bathroom and back, getting ready for their errands. In my sleep, I apparently tossed and turned myself into the doorway of the hallway, the only egress from the bedrooms and bathroom into the living room and the front door. And my head and shoulders fully blocked the exit to the living room.

I felt their footfalls approach and retreat from where I lay. Mom lightly click-clacking in her high heels, Dad's more substantial footfall only slightly diminished by his sneakers. I expected him to crush my head beneath his New Balance cross-trainers every time he made a pass. I detected a slowing each time either of them passed. I pretended to be asleep. To wake up would mean talking with them.

On what turned out to be the final pass, Dad's footfall slowed up. I held my breath. I heard him—or more precisely felt him—bend over. I held my breath waiting for him to back hand or head butt me. As he neared, I felt him reach to the blanket that had slid below my waist. He grunted—not an angry grunt, just one of a sixty-year-old man bending over—as he lifted the blanket over my shoulders. He placed his hand on my head, as close to tossing my hair as I'd ever experienced him doing, and then stepped over me to get to the door. That was it for Dad. The only other thing he ever said directly to me about my sexuality was that I should be careful about the deadly disease. It was 1985 when I came out, and AIDS was becoming part of the common discourse. I was still scared shitless, but I took his covering me up and his attempt at tenderness as a positive sign. I do today, for sure.

Mom, more in character, kicked me not so gently with the point of her high heels to move out of her way. She carried baby Johnny, my nine month old nephew, in her arms and told me—still in full high Moro princess regalness—to watch him until they got back. It seems that Princess and the boys had vanished last night during Mom's and my singkil performance. Had I known, I'd have taken one of their beds. She sat him in the crook of my arm and left.

Joseph Fejeran

Per Diem

It's nine o'clock in the morning, on a Sunday, and I am rushing into the shower.

This is the first day of the first conference on the first trip that, for the first time, an employer has paid for me to attend. I am rushing to get ready.

I shouldn't be rushing.

Who schedules a conference on a *Sunday* at 9:00 a.m.?! Sundays are reserved for Our Lord, Jesus Christ, and fabulous brunches. Since I haven't been keeping in touch with the former, I figure the latter should not be forgotten. So, I ordered a delicious room service spread to start my day: scrambled eggs with bacon, hashbrowns, a toasted English muffin with marionberry jam (because the only jam you should ever need is one named after Richie Cunningham's mother), and a side of orange juice to drink.

My wardrobe for the day, more like for the week, has been laid out and pressed from the moment the suitcase unzipped. I brought with me three pairs of shoes—options for casual, smart-casual and dressy—with me on this trip, which caused my checked bag to be six-point-five pounds over the limit, forcing me to empty its contents into a spare duffel bag, which I packed for just this scenario.

I shouldn't be rushing.

My name badge is placed on top of my notebook and next to my water bottle so I don't forget it. Apparently, you need to wear it all the time, or else they won't let you into the sessions, or worse, the lunches. I've even picked out the pen that I'm going to use: a Cross ballpoint. Its heavy thickness makes me feel like what I write to be of grave importance. Both the pen and my notebook are gifts from my family, engraved with my name, tokens of best wishes for the new job. My conference booklet, already bleeding blue from my note-taking, is placed next to a sweater and an umbrella. The forecast calls for rain, and though I will be indoors for most of this trip, you're never fully prepared unless you have an umbrella at the ready.

But all of my preparation is turning out to be a waste. I'm still rushing, not because I'm worried I'll be late. No, I am certain that I will be late, if not missing entirely, the first session of my first adult conference. I'm rushing into the shower because a guy I just met online is coming over to my hotel room. He's coming over, at 9:00 am, and we're going to get naked. He's going to be here in ten minutes.

After landing at the airport the day before, checking in to the hotel and exploring the city for a few hours, I decided, like I always do when I am in a new city, to check out the local talent. Ironically, around the New Year, I had publicly proclaimed the end of my search for a boyfriend. The manhunt was over, with no success whatsoever. I deactivated my accounts and deleted all my apps. No more Right Swipes. No more Adams. No more double-tapping jockstrap, bathroom mirror selfies. No more headless torsos and faceless cocks only looking for "friendship." No more Vers/Top MWMs that are VGL, HWP, DDF, HIV neg (u be 2), Cut and into WS. No more smiles, or winks, or pokes. No more "No Fats! No Femmes!" No more "masc4masc only." If I wanted any growling or woofing, I'd have to go to Michael Vick's backyard. I gave it all up. Cold turkey.

But it doesn't count if I'm not in my hometown, right?

Fuck it, I think to myself. Maybe, I'll have better luck out here. Maybe the scales of attractiveness are weighted differently in this state, and where I was a 6 back home, I could be a 7-8, or an out-of-town 9.

With a press of a button, *BLIP* goes the Grindr. Off the bench, and back in the game.

I spent the rest of that night online, indiscriminately messaging guys. When you're this struck by lust, any decent looking pic taken in halfway decent lighting is worth a message. My grandpa was a fisherman and taught me that if you cast enough lines, eventually you get a bite. But after a couple of hours of unresponsive messages, I was starting to give up.

Just as I was about to give up, I refreshed the page and saw a new, familiar face in the app. I recognized him immediately. I noticed him from earlier in the day as we were waiting at the front desk to check in. He was tall—at least 6'3"—but his posture was slightly hunched forward as if all his life he was surrounded by shorter people and ducked down as not to inconvenience them, or make them think any less of themselves. Height is not a requirement for me as much as it is for other people. I tend to like more practical things. Like a good smile, or a juicy butt. I noticed that he had both of those. His most noticeable quality was his hair. Buzzed on the sides nice and tight, with the length on the top slicked back. It was also bleached and then colored to a shade of blue somewhere between Serenity and Glacier. Not an easy look to get away with. But he wore it with such aplomb, that I could not help but be drawn to him.

I thought that he might just be another guest at the hotel. But shortly after the lobby sighting, I saw him again later at the first-timers' welcome reception. Not only was this tall, handsome man a guest at the hotel, but he was also attending the conference. I didn't talk to him then, as I was too focused on the unique networking opportunity this function represented, and I thought that I would express my desire into a tissue later that evening.

So imagine my good fortune to discover the Tall Man's smiling face staring back at me from my phone, little green dot telling me he's awake, and less than 650 feet away. I sent him my usual bait—Hi! *smiley-face-emoji* I'm Joe. How are you today?—and left it there.

Before long, I fell asleep and woke up unsatisfied and tumescent. Checking my phone, I noticed and didn't get a response until about eight forty-five this morning.

"Hi, Joe! I'm Cody. How's your morning going?" I saw that he was still online, so I replied right away.

Okay, I guess. Say, I think we're here for the same conference.

"Yeah! I think we are. I thought you looked familiar *smiley-face-emoji*"

Well, this is a little awkward. Meeting on here like this …

"Not awkward at all *winking-face-emoji* I just finished getting dressed myself."

Now for escalation…

Say, I don't know what your plans are for the day, but maybe we could grab some lunch or something?

"I'd be down to meet up *winking-face-emoji*" That response would have been enough for me to count this one in the "WIN" column, but then it was his turn to escalate.

"What are you up to now?" he typed. I replied with a raised eyebrow.

Just finished breakfast. Nothing like room service on the per diem to start things off right.

"Cool. Mind if I swing by?"

Sure. *Um. Duh, of course.* Here's my room number.

"Be there in a sec *smiley-face-emoji*"

Which brings me back to rushing into the shower. After having washed all of the important areas, I quickly dry myself off and swish with some mouthwash. I put on a sweater and some jeans, an act that is mired in futility as much as it is politeness.

I realize as I hurriedly straighten out my sheets and clean the room service tray, that most normal people have this notion that hookups happen under a cloak of darkness. That somehow, the night and all that it connotes about the unknown justifies the sub rosa nature of anonymous sex. Two consenting adults should know better than to flaunt their shamed craving in the light of day!

I guess that makes me a rebel, as a glass of half-finished OJ and remnants of an English muffin are about to witness things that typically take place the evening prior to their consumption. The sheer gluttony of my situation is not lost on me. It was not enough to order a meal of dubious fiscal responsibility, but that I could still fit one more thing inside me.

I hear a shuffling outside my door.

Tall Man knocks three times. He must want me.

I open the door, and he is even more delectable from zero feet away. I welcome him in with a flourished gesture that is typically reserved for hosts of HGTV shows. His smile catches my eye immediately. It has a genuinely mischievous quality to it. I did not jump on this man the moment he walked in because I am still not sure if I have read in between the lines correctly. I lay on the bed, and get comfortable, and he stands there next to me. We make the deferential small talk that you make. I learn that he's from the Bay Area, and has a side-hustle giving massages. I'm not sure if he gives *those* kinds of massages, but rent is too damn high up there. I also learn that he went out last night to a full-nude, male strip club.

"I called my husband to tell him what I was doing," he said. Cue record scratch sound effect. "He was so jealous! Even told me to get a lap dance."

Wow. How… understanding of him.

Now, I do not have a problem with messing around with a guy that is partnered/married. If they have an open arrangement, and they are honest about everything, then what is the big deal? I'm not under any delusion that I'm going to find the Next Great Love of My Life on a hook-up app. This is for him what it is for me: a bit of out-of-town fun. Nothing more.

At the inevitable lull in the conversation, Tall Man looks at me, then at his crotch, and back at me, smiling his shit-eating grin the whole time. It's this exchange that makes me nostalgic for a time that I was never a part of. When cruising meant going to smoke-filled bars with pitch-black back rooms. The time before online profiles, when the only push notifications you could receive was the trade grinding against you on the dance floor, and the only guy taking dick pics was Robert Mapplethorpe. A time when a simple look, a glance, a nod of the head was an elaborate semiotic language of desire. It was a time when advances and rejections were not as easily as ignored, because a flesh and blood person was standing in front of you, and not a headless digital image.

Tall Man makes eyes at me and leads my gaze toward his jeans. I begin to unbutton his jeans. (My *God*, do I *love* a button-fly pair of jeans.) One by one, until finally, I reveal his tumescence.

Oh, wow.

"Yeah. I know," says the Tall Man, eyes closing, shit-eating grin disappearing. "Get to it."

It's 9:00 a.m. on Sunday, the first day of my first adult conference for work, and I am going to miss the first two sessions. Once again, my best-laid plans are foiled by a lack of self-control.

I guess there's always tomorrow.

Marcel Monroy

days like lost dogs

Take me
tied
behind the woodshed
Put me down
beneath the dirt
Bury the bones deep so
the dogs don't dig them up
Salt the earth above
Savor the ripe flesh
Sentient meat
spoils
quicker than the rest
and the lye
will not deceive the air
of my scent
forever

Marcel Monroy

It will be for me
and I will want It

Sometimes I need taking
and/or
talking to.

You know this,
when it's time.
Or when
it will be,
for me.

Sometimes I need spanking
and/or
spit too.

I know this
won't fit,
but in time
it will
be for me.

Sometimes I need beating
and/or
barking too.

We know this abuse
would say,
could it speak,
it will be for me.

Marcel Monroy

Cherry

You swallowed
the whole cherry

even the pit

You tied the stem
with your tongue
into a knot
     a noose
     a necklace
then tightened it
with your teeth
around my neck

Marcel Monroy

well worn

if I do not fit you
force it,
walk with my rotted sole
trodden black beneath,
red tongue torn out,
laces tied back into
double knotted snake dens
brace me,
when you are done
unlace me.

Frank DiPalermo

Perverted and Possessed

In the seventies my family became deeply involved in the Charismatic Movement, which was how Catholics did born-again Christianity. We went to prayer meetings, read the bible, and glory-hallelujahed all over each other. When I came home from Mrs. Moon's sixth grade class, I often walked in on my mom and her friends having a prayer session in the family room. Mom was quite social and had her Christian chums over for coffee a couple of afternoons a week. Sometimes between one bite of crumb cake and the next, the Holy Spirit would fall upon them. It would urge them to start singing in tongues and lift their arms so they could do jazz hands for Jesus.

I frequently joined in. I was what, eleven years old? I was painfully awkward and so socially inept that I seemed to alienate people my own age just by breathing. The only place I felt truly comfortable was in the company of middle-aged suburban women, particularly if they were praising the Lord. The only time I was absolutely certain I wasn't committing a terrible sin without even realizing it was when

I was praying in the secret language God gave me when I received the baptism in the Holy Spirit. In other words, when I was speaking in tongues. I had a lot to pray for, because right around the time my first pubes sprouted, I became a nocturnal transgressor.

My first wet dream was not unexpected. I had sex-ed in school and a truly tortured conversation with my dad a few weeks after that. I knew all about the gooey mechanics of sex. What had me completely gobsmacked was the fact that my first wet dream was about Ned, the nerdy boy with the chipped front tooth who lived around the corner.

Calling this a dream didn't do it justice. This was a multi-sensory hallucination of creative carnality. I could actually feel what happened. And it was amazing, stuff I'd maybe heard of but couldn't convince myself two people really did together.

At one point in the dream I said (quite sexily, I'm sure), "Just let me put in the tip."

Ned responded, "Okay, but if I don't like it you have to stop." This turned out to be a prophetic moment as I had many real-world iterations of this conversation after I hit my twenties.

Here's the thing: until my first wet dream I had no idea, no fucking clue, that I was attracted to Ned. Until that dream, I had no idea that I was gay.

I tried to convince myself it was a fluke. I'd heard that young men early in puberty went through phases. But the dream about Ned turned out to be the first of many, many, many, many, many, many, many such dreams. Each one propelled me into a realm of electrically erotic, delightfully depraved, lasciviously sensual toe-curling intensity. When the time came for the wet part of the dream, I didn't just dribble, I achieved escape velocity. I swear, I could change the channel on my little black-and-white TV from across the room.

All of my wet dreams were about men. I dreamt about John, the tall blond kid who lived on Fernwood Drive. Which was followed by a dream about Ron, a bully at my school who completely terrified me, but was also kind of gorgeous. Which was followed by a dream about Tom, one of the few jocks who was actually a very sweet guy. Which was followed by a dream about Mr. Prepard, the Physical Education instructor. Which was followed by a dream. Which was followed by a dream. Which was followed by a dream. I had exactly one wet dream about a woman. Cher.

Faggot. Queerboy. Homo. Fairy. These were names I'd been called my whole life. The dreams made me realize that the people calling me those names were right.

How did I become an ungodly eleven-year-old? How did I become so wicked? How could things get any worse?

My mom developed a friendship with Kathy, a woman with shoulders like a linebacker who seemed amazingly tall to eleven-year-old me. She had a heavily pock-marked face, dyed-black hair combed into a Laura Petrie flip, and she smoked Salem cigarettes. Listening to her talk made me uncomfortable, because her voice sounded like it started too far back in her throat and her words were thick and spitty.

She and my mother got real close, real fast, so close Kathy felt it was within her rights to criticize me whenever she saw fit. Actually, Kathy felt it was within her rights to criticize anyone because she always knew what was best. For everyone. All the time.

Once, Kathy was at the kitchen table with Mom and she stopped me as I was heading out for a bike ride. "Frank, the Lord has given me a message for you." Her half-swallowed voice made the skin on my forearms shrink. "He does not like that shirt you're wearing." She was talking about a t-shirt my sister gave me for my birthday with an image of a flying eyeball on it. "That shirt is *of the devil*. You should burn it."

Hearing the phrase *of the devil* gave me gooseflesh. I'd snuck in to see *The Exorcist* a few years before, and thought of it more as a cautionary documentary than a horror movie. Which is not to say I wasn't terrified. Nothing scared me more than the devil, that random and marauding evil being who made Linda Blair do all those unspeakable things to herself. I immediately pulled that shirt off and did what Kathy said. I burned it in my dad's barbeque.

Here's what I didn't realize about Kathy: she was a horrible, miserable, angry, vindictive, spiteful woman who was probably starved for love, affection, and good sex. She gossiped constantly, viciously, and gussied-up her attacks as pious Christian concern. She tried to turn our entire prayer community against Patricia, a sweet and caring woman who did volunteer work for various Catholic charities. It wasn't until years afterward that I figured out the likely reason for this hostility. Patricia was the only woman in our prayer community who spoke with a Mexican accent.

Kathy was clearly a sadistic, judgemental creep. Why did anyone listen to her?

I think I figured that out, too. Kathy knew her audience. She carried a small tattered bible in her purse along with her Salem cigarettes and laid it on the table next to her coffee cup. She didn't read from it, not that I ever saw, just had it as a prop. She had this school-marmish manner that convinced people (by people, I mean me) whatever she said was for their own good. Whenever Kathy ripped into someone for singing too prettily in prayer meeting, laughing too loud, or being too sweet to their grandmother (no kidding, these are actual criticisms I heard her make), whenever Kathy was getting ready to shred you and leave you bleeding she always prefaced it with, "The Lord Jesus has given me a message for you."

Besides giving her messages, God apparently used Kathy as a kind of demon-detector. My flying eyeball t-shirt was a case in point but there were plenty of other examples. One warm spring day, I came home from school to find a roaring fire in the fireplace. My mom and Kathy were tossing things into it. Kathy said that sculptures and drawings of frogs or owls were *of the devil.* I asked Kathy why. She said, "Owls and frogs are the only animals in all of creation that hunt at night."

Bullshit. Bats, hedgehogs, jaguars, leopards, raccoons, rats, mice, tarantulas, foxes, a million animals hunted at night and I knew it. But it was easier to make myself believe Kathy's words than to consider the possibility that a Catholic Charismatic could be dead wrong, loony, or even malicious.

Kathy went on to say that any artistic representations of owls or frogs were little portals that allowed Satan a way into the home of otherwise upstanding Christians like us.

I helped Mom and Kathy go through the entire house. We collected every offending artifact we could find, a plastic froggy soap dish, a drawing of a bunch of owls on a branch with the last one hanging upside down and the words "Nobody's Perfect" printed underneath, and a cutesy green candle in the shape of a frog on a lily pad that one of our neighbors gave Mom for watering their houseplants when they went on vacation. We fed that tacky crap into the fire, said a few prayers, and slammed the door on Satan.

But demons didn't rely solely on kitschy owls and frogs. Evil spirits could find all kinds of ways into your life.

Another time I came home from school, and it wasn't just Kathy and my mom. Gloria was there, too. Gloria was a very sweet Italian lady who wore her hair in a low-key bouffant even though it was the seventies and everyone else was doing the blow-dry thing. She was sitting in a chair in the middle of the family room holding a spaghetti pot in her lap. Why was Gloria holding a spaghetti pot in her lap? Mom and Kathy stood behind her with their hands on her shoulders. All of them had their eyes pinched shut and they were singing in tongues so loud and so fast that sometimes spit flew out of their mouths. Gloria rocked back and forth in her chair. Between frenetic bursts of prayer language, she moaned and groaned like she was sick at her stomach. The whole room crackled. I was afraid to touch the walls because I might get electrocuted. I wouldn't have been surprised if lightning struck and took out our couch.

All of a sudden, Kathy said as loudly as her throttled voice would allow, "Evil spirit, I bind you with the word of God. In the name of Jesus, I command you, come out of Gloria."

An honest-to-god exorcism. In our family room. Neat.

Gloria threw back her head and opened her mouth. And her voice. Wow. In *The Exorcist*, when the devil took hold of Linda Blair, her voice turned all gravelly and raspy and twisted. It was so terrifying it made my hair stand up straight. Gloria, a forty-ish lady from the suburbs, sounded like she was doing a really lame imitation of that. Her demon said, "I will come out. I will come out. I will come out. And I will go into the child."

Gloria's demon voice may have been cheesy, but it also scared the crap out of me because Gloria wasn't faking. No one was faking. Something real and strange and terrifying was happening. And it wasn't just happening to Gloria. Because the child that demon wanted to go into? That was me.

Then Gloria puked. Not a lot. Not projectile. Not pea soup green. But still, Gloria puked. In Mom's spaghetti pot.

That was fucked up.

I sprinted out of there. I made the mistake of going to my room instead of outside. I heard the rest of the exorcism through the two-by-fours and drywall of our home. Which was so much worse because it made the walls and doors of the house seem like flimsy protection from an evil spirit who just announced he was gunning for me.

Kathy kept saying, "In the name of Jesus, I cast you out! In the name of Jesus, I cast you out. In the name of Jesus!" My mom sang in tongues louder and faster and faster and louder and you can bet she still had one hand on Gloria's shoulder while the other was doing spastic and spiritual jazz hands. Gloria's demon didn't talk anymore, just kind of barked like a raspy little chihuahua. This went on for I don't know how long. Then, silence.

This next part just killed me. Kathy, Gloria and my mom started to laugh. My mom said, "Well. That was something."

Laughing? They just turned the demon loose! Where did they think he was gonna go? I don't know, maybe the timid little homo hiding out in his bedroom? I could feel the evil spirit in the crawl space, curling like smoke around the joists and floorboards, prodding and poking, trying to find a way into my room. Holy Crap. The heating vent. I closed it but that couldn't possibly be enough. So, I put my open bible over it. Then I sneaked into the guest room where my mom kept the extra crucifixes. Yeah, I lived in a house with a drawer full of extra crucifixes. I propped one over my door and another over the window. Then what? Maybe I should stuff a towel under the door? Can terrycloth stop a demon? I would have strung up a bunch of garlic, but that was just a silly superstition.

One of the pictures my mom hung in the hallway fell off the wall. Honestly, this wasn't the first time that picture took a dive. It was really big with a heavy frame and my mom had it hanging by two thumbtacks. Literally, two thumbtacks. But this time, when that picture fell, I was certain it had nothing to do with physics or gravity. I was wrong earlier. The demon wasn't in the crawl space. He was much too brazen for that. He was traipsing right down the hallway, raking his fingers along the wall, sparks flying from the end of his talons. I wouldn't have been surprised if that painting burst into flames before it hit the ground. I got so freaked out I jammed myself into the closet and wedged my Vans and Connie Allstars under the door. Then I waited. And listened. And waited. And listened. And waited. And waited.

I discovered the problem with a really good hiding place. How did you know when to come out? Plus, this demon just left a sweet little Italian lady from the suburbs, the only kind of person I ever felt safe around. Now, he was rambling somewhere in my house. Who would I feel safe around now? Where would I feel safe? Would I ever feel safe?

The honest answer was no, I wouldn't. I was a scared and closeted gay boy who had wet dreams about Ned, the nerdy kid with the chipped front tooth that lived around the corner. My home was filled with a bunch of Catholic Charismatics who went to prayer meetings, read the bible, sang in tongues, cast out demons, and voted a straight Republican ticket. It was never going to be safe to come out of the closet.

Eventually, I had no choice. Hunger and a filled-to-bursting bladder were my downfall. I crept out of my closet and then my room. Chicken cacciatore was simmering in the kitchen. Gloria and Kathy were gone, the picture was back on the wall, and Mom was humming "You Light Up My Life" as she stood at the stove. Everything seemed normal but I was as flinchy as a cat. Was the demon hiding in the statuette of a little girl with a frilly parasol? What about that painting of a lady with one boob hanging out of her toga? I know Satan likes representations of owls and frogs, but how does he feel about blue and white ceramic salt shakers with paintings of windmills on them? The devil could be absolutely anywhere and watching out for him exhausted me. Everything got worse once the sun went down. I got through that long and terrifying night by leaving the light on, sleeping in fits and starts, and masturbating without restraint.

Surprisingly, entire weeks went by with no one speaking in a weird evil voice, no one throwing up in mom's spaghetti pot, and no demons threatening to invade my soul. The everydayness of things soothed me. I began to lose the sense of being stalked by evil. Our house started to feel like a home, not a hidey-hole for Satan. I relaxed. Then, a couple of months after the exorcism extravaganza, my mom had Kathy over for coffee again. She and Mom were sitting in the kitchen when I came home from school.

It was a lazy afternoon for them. No burning of unholy images. No casting out of evil spirits. Just coffee and gossip. I walked past the kitchen and heard Kathy say to my mom, "You know homosexuality is more than a sin. The gays are possessed by the evil spirit of homosexuality. Until they are delivered of this demon, God will smite them to hell, and they will never enter the kingdom of heaven."

I didn't cry when I heard this. I couldn't. How would I explain myself? I went to my room, started reading Batman comics, and pretended I wasn't bothered. But I'd been gutted. The thought of spending eternity cut off from the people and the God I loved was unbearable, shameful, and heartbreakingly lonely. That day, I took on a secret and grinding burden that I would not put down for many years.

That was the last bit of spiritual venom Kathy would spit in my direction. Shortly afterward she moved away, and my mom lost track of her.

Fast forward to now. I'm about to turn fifty-eight. In my distant past are years of colon-twisting, agonizing struggle. I tried as hard as I could to not be gay, even harder to be a good Christian. But it was pointless. I simply am queer. I simply am not Christian.

Giving up Christianity was like pulling out a loose baby tooth, there was a quick twinge of pain and then this small, brittle, fragile thing that had long outlived its usefulness was gone. It was replaced with something stronger and bigger and better. It was replaced with me, strange and insecure and damaged. Loving and ballsy and athletic, creative and loyal and outdoorsy—I am all this and a Walt-Whitman-multitude of other things, but mostly, ardently, uniquely and sometimes still timidly, I am queer.

I am.

Queer.

I've been with a wonderful man for over thirty years and we've been married since 2014. I live an imperfect, but mostly great life. I'm thankful for that. But sometimes, I look back on the time when I struggled so hard to be something I wasn't, a time when I believed I was spiritually doomed. Sometimes, I look back on the people who made that time so much harder than it needed to be. Sometimes I look back on Kathy. I have something I want to say to her and I'm going to say it right now:

Fuck you, Kathy. Fuck you.

Melia Lenkner

Two Girls on a Rainy Evening

Nighttime and October rain are fresh in the air. We linger in
the driveway, just outside the porchlight's reach, reluctant to
re-enter; my hand lingers in hers.

We have just recently discovered the joys of kissing, and,
pressed close by the intimacy of a shared umbrella, the
unspoken question is soft in her brown eyes: *"Here?"*

My back is to the porchlight, but the brightness lingers on
my skin; it aches like day-old sunburn.

I kiss her hand in compromise, remove it from my own.

We return indoors.

Mickey Brent

Cookies At Lisa's

It was late summer. School had just started. I was a
first-year college student, and not quite eighteen. I sat
across from Lars, my boyfriend, in the dorm cafeteria. As
usual, we were inhaling our dinners after our study break,
which was a daily five-mile run. All pumped up and sweaty,
we'd rush into the cafeteria to scarf down our "carbs and
veggies" before hitting the books again. Such typical, young
Californians.

But that night, I stopped mid-chew as my eyes spotted a
girl across the room. A guy was leaning into her. *Cute couple,*
I thought, studying their handsome faces. Then I felt a knot
in my throat. I couldn't tell if it was my burger or the girl. She
had on a snug white T-shirt. My heart was pounding, and I
kept staring at her. I had no idea what was going on. My chest
burst with emotions. *Envy?* Sure, her boyfriend was cute... but
so was mine. *No.* It had to be the girl. Something radiated from
her, zapping all the cells in my body.

I chewed my burger as I studied her. She had dark cropped
hair, with a small, long tail in the back. *She's so unique. So daring.
So strong.* After running five miles, I'd been pooped, but at that

moment I felt revved up, as if she were a heavy-duty battery. I felt an intense pull toward her.

I'd love for us to be friends.

Often, after seeing that girl in the cafeteria, I found myself daydreaming about her. I'd close my eyes and my mind would explore her face, hair, athletic body... even the unique tone of her voice as she laughed during meals with her lively crew of friends. I'd push aside my books, letting my thoughts seep into a tangy field of intrigue. I felt as if she were a luscious flower and I were a thirsty bee.

I finally discovered her name: Lisa.

I learned her boyfriend's, too, which I conveniently forgot.

Lars and I always ran in silence on our long, afternoon "study breaks." That's probably why he failed to pick up on my increasingly frequent mental lapses. I daydreamed so often about Lisa that I began to fear the worst. *Am I a pervert?* I'd wonder as our sneakers tore through the autumn leaves. I'd conjure up scenes where I'd run smack into her—in the library, the gym, or on the dance floor.

I couldn't wait for our dorm's Saturday-night dance parties. My eyes would scan the door until Lisa and her boyfriend showed up, dressed in identical outfits: tight black jeans and white open-buttoned dress shirts. Lars guzzled microbrews with our buddies while I secretly focused on Lisa, who danced so hard, her white shirts quickly turned transparent. I secretly admired her chest muscles as the wet cotton stretched across her broad shoulders.

Live concerts were even better. She'd shake and grind in such a frenetic state, sweat flew from her tail like wild pearls. I'd shut my eyes and imagine it trickling down my hot cheeks. I basked in this fantasy while Lisa escaped to change into a fresh shirt. I wondered how anyone could be so energetic, talented, and wild, for hours on end. But I was way too shy to introduce myself. Besides, she hadn't noticed me. I was sure of that. Finally, these incessant thoughts made me so anxious, my life spun out of control. The highs hit each time I saw Lisa. I felt so excited and alive, my thoughts would race, and my stomach would churn like butter. Especially at night—I'd spend hours imagining a chance encounter. Heart pounding and skin sticking to my sweaty sheets, I no longer cared about midterms or track meets. I began questioning my relationship with Lars. He was a perfect catch: nice, cute, smart. But secretly, all my thoughts revolved around Lisa. I panicked.

How can I feel so strongly about someone I've never even met? How long is this obsession going to last?

I wondered about my sexuality. I'd spent years trying to figure out who I was, *what* I was, while torturous, existentialist thoughts kept me up at night. I was convinced I'd been baked from a different mold than other human beings. I didn't know anyone like me who secretly desired people I couldn't have. I was a freak of nature. A mess-up. That was my dark, childhood secret.

Sure, I'd read about gay people. As a former competitive tennis player, I'd heard some pretty awful locker room stories about how gay, lesbian, and trans professional tennis players were treated. Homophobia formed a large part of my upbringing. Intellectually, I didn't want to be different. Inside, however, I knew I was, but I continued to fight it over the years.

Finally, to my relief, when my freshman year ended, things returned to normal. Summer came and went. My relationship with Lars had lost its flavor, like an over-chewed stick of gum. Lars transferred to another university; our breakup proved too painful for him. I was just a normal, busy sophomore and I'd nearly forgotten about Lisa. I started dating other guys—nothing serious—and my life was running smoothly.

Until Lisa showed up in my psychology class.

My life went haywire after I noticed her sitting on the other side of the auditorium. After that, I always snagged a chair at least three rows away from her. I wanted to stay away, yet still be able to peek at her. The intrigue was still there. In fact, it was torture. My heart kept pounding, making it impossible for me to concentrate. I needed to pass the class, but she kept making things so difficult. And I didn't even know her!

One day, after another boring psychology lecture, I rose from my chair to see Lisa standing inches from my nose. Her smile revealed sparkling, healthy teeth. I froze.

"Hi! I'm Lisa. What are you doing after class? Wanna come over and bake cookies?"

I tried to conceal my surprise. I'd never even talked to her before, and here she stood, hands on her slim hips, asking me to her place. *She's inviting me over to bake cookies. Me!*

My eyes locked with the inquisitive green pair before me and I heard myself blurt out, "I'd love to." Grabbing my books, I nearly tripped over myself as I followed her from the lecture hall.

Ten minutes later, we parked our bikes in front of a quaint, gray house. *She's so cool.* I cringed at the thought of my tiny dorm room and annoying roommate. My eyes traced the contours of Lisa's body as she bent over to lock her bike. I blushed and looked away with embarrassment as pages of my past returned to the first time I ever saw her.

I couldn't figure out what I was doing on her doorstep. My throat was parched and I was too moved to say anything. Awkwardly, I followed her inside. She turned to face me. The tension between us was so thick, I could've poked a hole in it. It was like that static electricity I used to get on family trips to

Arizona. Each time I stepped on the carpet my hair shot up. If I touched something metallic—or even non-metallic, like my brother—sparks flew.

Sparks were flying now. I clenched my fists behind my back. Lisa flashed me a smile. "Want to see a tour of the house?" I nodded, feeling that familiar knot in my throat.

Her house was well-worn, yet cozy. I spotted a cracked leather sofa on a homespun rug. The air smelled of Indian incense and cut flowers—hardly a typical students' manor.

Grinning, Lisa led me into the kitchen and showed me all her handmade pottery.

I ran my finger over an earthy, rustic bowl. *So unique. Just like you. But when do you have time to pinch pots?* Before I could ask her, she opened the freezer.

"Time to get to work." She cut a roll of frozen cookie dough into little round portions, placed them on cookie sheets, popped them into the oven, and set the timer for forty-five minutes.

"Now, time to finish the tour," she declared. "Next stop, my bedroom..."

I gulped.

Lisa ushered me into a small, dimly lit bedroom with colorful, collaged walls and multi-dimensional mirrors. Then she plopped down on an oversized bed that took up half the room.

"Don't just stand there." She tapped a spot on the bedspread next to her.

I hesitated. Then I was hit with a flash of intuition, like driving through a tunnel and *smack*, I was on the other side. A burst of light blinded me as I moved through the darkness and a zillion sensations took over my body. *Holy crap!* I realized what was happening. This was no normal, innocent cookie-baking afternoon. Lisa had carefully arranged this. The cookies were her bait, and I was the innocent mouse. *I'm so naïve.* She wanted me to sit next to her so she could *kiss* me! *But she still has that boyfriend and... wait, I have one too. Or do I?* My mind was muddled. I couldn't remember if I had a boyfriend. Heck, I couldn't even remember my name.

Somehow, despite my deep reservations, I ended up sitting next to Lisa on the bed. All I could focus on was her, and how much my body was trembling. My awareness heightened even more. I heard her breath: shallow and quick, matching my racing heartbeat. Strange emotions swarmed my body. Time stopped.... Our shoulders touched, creating a static spark. Yet we weren't in Arizona. She wasn't my brother. It was Lisa, magnificent Lisa, and we were in her bedroom, together. And we didn't even know each other. Two complete strangers in a funky house, mid-afternoon, sharing extremely intimate space—on a huge bed—with eighteen chocolate chip cookies baking in the oven.

Moments like these only come once in a lifetime.

My tongue stuck to the back of my teeth. My gut raged as hot sensations surged through my body. *Should I obey my natural desires? Or shut it all off?*

Damn. All those wasted years, wondering who I was, *what* I was. When I finally got the chance to find out, I didn't know if I should take it, or stub it out, like a toxic, burning cigarette. Irrational thoughts raced through my mind. Wasn't it safer to dispose of my fantasy—with its rollercoaster emotions and sensuous imaginings—and keep within the limits of societal conformity and heterosexuality? I grew up thinking it was better to lock up my secrets and chuck the key.

I felt Lisa's warm breath on my shoulder and I tensed up. *I can't take this anymore.* I wanted to numb my body, and my attraction to Lisa.

Kill it, kill it! I ordered myself.

Painfully, the seconds ticked by. Panicking, I imagined my hot cheeks and tender body, like a steak about to be devoured by a ravenous lion. *Lisa's the animal, and I'm the prey.*

"I'm really sorry, but I've... got to go," I stammered, springing from the bed.

Lisa's face registered surprise, yet she licked her lips with a devilish grin. "But you haven't even tried the cookies! They're almost ready.... Please stay!" She grabbed my arm.

Head spinning, I jerked away. It's fight, flight, or freeze. I've got to escape—this bedroom, this girl, and her scary, weird house. I raced out of the bedroom, banging my shin on the kitchen table as I grabbed my backpack.

I didn't even notice the pain. Until I heard a scream.

I froze. I thought it was my scream. Or maybe Lisa's.

Then I realized it was the oven timer. The whole place smelled like cookies. Sickly sweet, bubbling hot, chocolate chip cookies. I felt nauseous and wanted to throw up.

Lisa shut off the timer and tried to tempt me with a cookie. I came up with a lame excuse about finishing my chemistry homework and ran out the door.

"Thanks! See ya," I shouted, pedaling as fast as I could until I passed four intersections. When I finally slowed down, my heart burst. I clenched the handlebars to keep from shaking. After a few deep breaths, I wiped the tears from my cheeks and pedaled on, wondering if I'd done the right thing, or if I'd just ruined the most incredible chance of my life.

I was so shaken that afternoon at Lisa's. At the time, I didn't regret my decision to leave. Not right away. But later on, I did. I dreamed of acting on my true desire to let Lisa kiss me, hold me tightly in her arms, tackle me on the bedspread—and let her burn the cookies. What would've happened to my life if I'd caved in?

I told myself that if I *had* surrendered, I probably would've flunked out of school. There was no way I could've kept studying with her lurking around. I'd have been too tempted to watch her make pinch pots, touch her short, spiky hair, run my fingers under her crisp, white dress shirt—translucent against her smooth, wet chest—while she danced for me. It would've been much more serious than dealing with burnt cookies. Given my fear of lesbians since childhood, due to my religious upbringing, and the fact that I had no real role model in those days, I probably would have emerged from the experience messed up inside.

I had no idea what to do with all my conflicting thoughts. For a long time afterwards, I suppose to protect myself as a vulnerable, budding lesbian, I conveniently blocked out the entire experience.

It took many years for me to grow comfortably into my own skin and find the right relationships, with both myself and other people. After experiencing so much confusion around my sexuality when I was younger, I finally found my life partner: an amazing woman. In fact, I became so confident in my role as a lesbian that I wrote articles for a queer newspaper in San Francisco, and then I became an author of lesbian romances for Bold Strokes Books.

Now, decades later, when I'm eating chocolate chip cookies, I think back on that strange Autumn day, wondering what would've happened if I'd stayed. I might have had a heart attack on her bed, due to my anxiety about being touched by her. Would I have slipped under the covers, like a submarine at sea, never to emerge from her muscular arms? Would she have ditched her boyfriend for me? Would we have ended up a loving couple? Maybe she just invited me over for a one-time experiment, like a tourist searching for cheap thrills, while she explored my shaking body—and the novelty of getting it on with another woman. When I sip milky tea out of my homemade mug—for I went on to create my own pinch pots, too—I wonder if Lisa still makes cookies for strangers, if she still has short hair with a long tail, if she still changes her sweaty shirts when dancing, if she ever married that boyfriend of hers, if she ever had kids, or if she ended up a happy, proud lesbian. Like me.

Paul Georgeades

Cold Turkey

When I was growing up, being gay was not an option. There were no out celebrities, no pop stars or politicians advocating for queer rights, no gay-themed TV shows. Homosexuality wasn't discussed, or even acknowledged, on the national stage. It was considered sick, disgusting, abnormal, tantamount to bestiality. There was simply no place for gays in mainstream society. Not surprisingly, a lot of people tried to lead straight lives.

My sexuality was especially confusing for me because I'd always had crushes on girls as a kid. When these crushes became exclusively same-sex when I got to high school, I blamed it on the fact that I went to an all-boys school. I assumed it was kind of like the prison effect. What any normal guy would do in such a situation. But when I got to college, things didn't change.

It was the fall of sophomore year and I was nineteen. I was sitting on the lawn by the soccer fields, studying with my friend John, when we were suddenly engulfed by the track team. We looked up as fifty runners jogged past.

"Shit, you see the tits on those two chicks on the end?" John smirked.

"Dude, totally."

But I hadn't seen them. All I saw was the two dozen lithe and shirtless boys. This disturbed me. Boys had been starring in my elaborate sexual fantasies for years, the sole target of my lust. But the idea that I could be gay was ludicrous. I thought musical theater was cheesy, I hated shopping, and I was slovenly. How could I be gay? I just had the misfortune of going to a Catholic high school. Clearly it had damaged me. I needed to correct the problem.

So I came up with a plan. I rationalized that the reason I wasn't pursuing girls was because I had another avenue: masturbation. From the time I was thirteen, I'd begun each morning and ended each night with a "cleaning of the pipes," so to speak, and it had sapped my motivation. If I could just stop jacking off, the desire would build up, and I'd be chasing after girls in no time. If I could eliminate this other outlet and make girls my only conduit to orgasm, I would resume my rightful place among straight men.

So the following day, I quit beating off, cold turkey.

Two weeks later, I was barely sleeping, I'd lost weight, and I would fly off the handle at the slightest thing. Much to my dismay, this little experiment had sharpened my lust for all the cute boys in my classes. But the worst had to be Tom Blesdoe. Tom had brown hair and brown eyes and really white skin, and an ass that was so tight and perky, it was prehensile. He was a perfect little twink. He was also what was referred to as, in technical terms, a douche. He wore a baseball cap backwards and had a penchant for throwing things (bottle caps, food) across a crowded room. We were in the same anthropology class, and though we didn't have much in common, we became friends because we both… well, because I wanted to fuck him. Every Tuesday and Thursday we studied together.

"You read what it said about the Sambia?" Tom asked. "The boys suck off the men to get strength from their semen. Disgusting. What a bunch of fags!"

"Maybe it works."

"Gross, dude. Can you imagine a whole fucking country of nothing but fags?"

"I… I've imagined that."

Tom closed his books and stood. "I'm gonna grab some 'za. You wanna come?"

"I'll meet you. I need to finish some reading."

It took fifteen minutes for the commotion in my pants to settle down enough for me to safely stand and leave the table. That night I lay awake, thinking about Tom's calves as I struggled to keep from touching myself.

A few weeks later, I was starting to lose it. I was constantly on edge, and I felt like a trap about to spring. I had to quit boxers and switch to briefs, wearing two pairs to tamp things down. Merely reading the letters T-O-M, in words like tomorrow, customer, optometrist, made me instantly hard. If someone had blown a little air in the direction of my crotch, I would have come my pants. However, I would not give in to temptation. Only with a girl would I allow myself to orgasm.

Then I met Evette. We had become friends through our political work, and though she had large hips and ample breasts, her hair was short and her face somewhat boyish. My strategy had worked! I did sorta maybe find her attractive, and the bumbling overtures I made seemed to be returned, so we started hanging out. We went to movies, dinner, and parties together. I enjoyed her company, but the end of the night was always an anxious, unbearable time. I knew from movies and television that this was the time when the man was expected to steal a kiss, when things progressed to "your place or mine;"

I needed to cross this milestone but I was clueless and felt woefully inadequate.

So I always found an excuse to dash off at the last minute. We'd be alone, the night winding down, and I could sense that Evette was waiting for me to make a move. Then I'd spot a bus pulling to the curb. "Shit, my bus!" I'd yell, bid a quick goodbye, and run off to catch it. There were always departing rides with friends I needed to take, unforeseen circumstances to suddenly pull me away, and if we were at a party, I would just secretly leave.

I was perturbed to discover that people had noticed we'd been hanging out and were asking questions. "What's up with you and Evette?" friends would inquire. I had assumed that my tentative and feckless stab at wooing a girl would be an embarrassment I'd stumble through privately. But it was turning into a very public matter. Everyone in our social circle seemed to know that nothing yet had happened, making the pressure to perform all the more acute.

In November, my house decided to have a potluck. I invited Evette over early to help me cook because I figured that's what a guy who's into a girl would do. We had fun making enchiladas. Soon, the guests arrived and my living room was filled with people.

I was standing with Evette, nibbling on some Swedish meatballs, when I noticed my housemate Sarah across the room. She was talking to her friend and looking our way. I became paranoid.

"Do you think they're gonna fuck?" I could have sworn I heard her say.

"Can he even handle it?" They both started laughing.

I looked around the room. Everyone seemed to be whispering and giggling as they glanced our way. Worse were the knowing and approving smiles.

I realized I had backed myself into a corner. In the past, I could always escape at the last minute, but now Evette was in my home. There would be nowhere for me to run. Tonight would have to be the night we did the deed. I would be trapped. The party would be clearing out and there she would be, along with my housemates, all waiting for me to make a move. It was not only that I had no desire to have sex with Evette—I was positively terrified of it. All the sex I had before was with boys and had taken place in my mind. One of the benefits of being homosexual is that you already have a lot of familiarity with the equipment. You've been taking it on test runs for years. But a vagina was a completely foreign entity. I hadn't the slightest clue what to do. There was no owner's manual, nothing to tell me what to expect.

I began to panic. Evette was saying something, but I couldn't hear. I excused myself to go to the bathroom but fled outside instead. What had I gotten myself into? I paced back and forth, nervous as hell, wondering if I should just leave, just hop on a bus and go to campus. Then an idea came to me. I'd get out of this just as I had with swimming lessons when I was seven years old.

I burst into the party, a look of pain on my face, and melodramatically announced:

"I just puked on the side of the house."

My friend Jonah came forward apologetically, and the bottle of wine he bought for a dollar was identified as the culprit. Sarah ushered me up to my room, fetching club soda to settle my stomach.

I lay on my bed listening to the party downstairs, waiting for it to end. When the last guests finally left, I heard someone ascending the stairs. My door swung open.

"Paul?" It was Evette.

A rush of fear tightened my stomach. *Please don't come inside, please don't come inside.*

The wood floor creaked as she stepped inside.

"Are you okay?"

"I feel like I'm gonna puke." I moaned in my sickliest voice.

"I'm leaving. I'll talk to you tomorrow."

I didn't speak to her the next day, and another week had passed. I had blown my chance. But I would not abandon my strategy, though something had to give. In my escalating desire and lack of sleep I had become careless, been a little too "hands-on" with Tom and some other boys. Snide comments were made, and eventually they'd start to catch on. I'd be exposed, ostracized, hated. There would be no denying that I was, in fact, this thing so universally reviled.

During Thanksgiving break, all my housemates went home, but I stayed. Evette was also in town, and I figured this would be my opportunity for a second chance, without anyone there to witness my ineptitude. I bought a bottle of wine and invited her over. A few hours later we were both drunk, and I found the courage to ask if she wanted to go to my room. She said yes. We climbed the stairs solemnly, and to me it felt not like two kids heading for a frolic in bed, but like to workmen ascending to clean the attic. Somehow we started kissing. We fell on the bed. Our shirts came off. I played with her breasts for a while, but I knew what I had to do. Flaccid, terrified, hands shaking, I moved to unbutton her jeans. But she stopped me. I tried to conceal my gratitude. I met her gaze. I saw fear in her eyes.

I looked at her uncommonly short hair, her man's shirt thrown on the floor. A thought entered my head: Evette was implementing the same strategy as me.

"I'm having my period," she said. "Let's just cuddle."

I searched her face but couldn't read anything more. The thought passed and my uncertainty returned.

"Sure," I said, trying to sound disappointed.

I lay down on the bed and put my arm around her. If Evette had said, "I'm a lesbian," as she in fact turned out to be, I would have felt relieved. We could have both relaxed and shared ourselves. We could have laughed, become confidantes, friends.

But Evette wasn't able to utter those words. I was unable to tell her the truth about how I felt. So we lay there in our tense embrace, feeling confused, inadequate, abnormal. Feeling that singular loneliness when you are forced to guard your heart, when you believe that you alone must fend off the world's revulsion and disgust.

Fifteen minutes later, Evette said she had to go and I was relieved. I walked her to the door and said goodbye. When the latch had clicked, I went immediately to the bathroom to fetch the lotion, thinking only of Tom; and at least for that moment, nothing else mattered.

Catherine Moscatt

The Girl with
The Magenta Hair

Jackie is only 9 but she spits
This homophobic hate speech
During lunch
My peanut butter and jelly sandwich
Looked like it got run over
By a bus
There's a handful of orange slices
For dessert
I roll my eyes at Kelly,
The girl with the magenta hair
And squeeze her hand a little
Harder
Under the table
They would flip if they saw it
So we make sure they won't
See us locking pinkies on the walk to the gym
She likes to draw pictures of us
Kissing except the girl she draws isn't me, that is
Some other girl comfortable in her
Sexuality, happy in her own skin

If that was me I don't think
I would be in this program at all
But I am
We both are
They like to label us as
Troubled, wild, crazy, take your pick
Too screwed up
For the halls of
High school we sit behind these locked doors
The girl with the magenta hair understands
Me like no one else
And that's why lunchtime is my
Favorite part of the day
We can play our favorite game called
Let's Pretend We are Anywhere but Here
Let's pretend to be normal
Let's pretend to be accepted
Our hands are sticky with orange juices,
Fingers still intertwined

Joel Castellaw

Two Are Better Than One

"**N**ow, Joel, logic should tell you that a mouth or an anus is no place for a penis."

That's my dad. He can be a little clinical. He is also pretty biblical. The earth is 6,000 years old. Noah really did get all those animals on the ark. Plagues of locusts. Leviticus 18:22, "Thou shalt not lie with mankind as with womankind; it is abomination," all that.

We were sitting under the fruitless mulberry tree in the backyard after dad picked me up from jail, where I had spent the night after being arrested for possession of psilocybin. As my parents asked questions trying to figure out what had gone wrong with their son, their baby, I sank deeper and deeper into my lawn chair and into my late-teen angst.

"Did this all start when you decided to wear black all the time? Did we make a mistake letting you join the drama club? It's those Gerhard boys' fault, isn't it?" I wanted, more than anything, for their questions to stop.

So, when Dad asked, "Why aren't you hanging around with the Christian kids anymore?" I told them, "Those kids don't want to hang out with me anymore because I'm gay," flinging the statement in their faces with spit and insolence. Their responses? My mom said, "You don't look gay." My dad snorted, "Well, we'll just have to fix that, too," and everything stopped. No more with the third-degree questions, no more probing. Just icy silence.

My parents never saw what they didn't want to see. Sweeping everything under the rug was an artform in my family. But how could they have not seen? I was the little boy who struck a princess pose on his roller skates while my brother and sister leaned forward on theirs like bad-ass hockey players.

When my dad tried to butch me up a little by getting me a football uniform when I was about seven, I was only interested in it as another opportunity to play dress-up. Did they really never notice me ogling the Greek statues of naked youth in Collier's Encyclopedia? "You don't look gay." At least it diverted their attention from the circumstances of my arrest. That didn't matter so much anymore. This was the real problem, that their kid was gay: "We'll just have to fix that, too."

So, a few days later, because coming out is never just a one-and-done conversation, there was the squirm-inducing talk with my dad where he got all clinical about what parts should naturally fit where (and where they shouldn't). "Logic should tell you, Joel, that God made the male and female sex organs so that they would go together. Homosexual relations are probably no worse than fornication, of course, but the point is that it just isn't pleasing in God's sight." My response to him was just as insolent as it had been a few days before: "Alright, if sex is just for making babies, what happens now that you and mom are too old to have any more kids?" He looked at me with disgust. We traded a few more jabs. I did not want to cave in to him and his lecture on the evils of homosexuality. But I was also a marginally employed eighteen-year-old in a jam. I was going to need his help to deal with the aftermath of having been arrested. So, when he said he wanted us all—him, Mom, and me—to go to counseling together, I agreed—not because I had any desire to make any changes in my life, but just in hopes that agreeing might make this whole nightmare go away.

We went to see a Christian family counselor—Dad's choice, of course. He looked sort of like a blonde Mr. Rogers, but with glasses and worse taste in sweater vests. The sessions were banal and unproductive. "Draw a picture of yourself in relation to your parents…. Don't pursue theatre in college—it's a hotbed of drug use and homosexuality…. Tell me about your experiences with girls."

"I've been with girls, and it's alright, but I just don't have the same feelings for them as I do when I kiss another guy."

I thought my response would shock him, but he just seemed perplexed. I realize today that it was all sort of an inept attempt at conversion therapy. My dad's a frugal guy, though, and after a handful of expensive visits that yielded no results, he quickly agreed when I said it wasn't doing anything for me and I wanted to stop.

He set up a weight-training routine for me, sure that I would give up the gay if he could just reform the sissy in me. "I'm sure if you can just put on some muscle, you'll develop more normal feelings about girls."

The effect was just the opposite of what he intended. As I lay back on the workout bench in the garage to pump some iron, I just ended up fantasizing more than ever about guys.

And, over time, we simply stopped talking about me being gay—another thing swept under the rug. Oh, and the arrest pretty much went away, too. I was eventually "sentenced" to diversion and informal probation. I don't know if the fact that

Dad was chief deputy probation officer of Orange County at the time has anything to do with why I got off so easily, but whatever it was I was happy to put the consequences behind me.

Four years went by with no discussion or acknowledgment of me being gay, and then it bubbled back up again. Mom was in her sewing room darning socks, wearing this contraption on her head with magnifying lenses attached to it to help her see and avoid poking herself with the needle. I was in the kitchen, and she called out to me: "Joel, come here. I need to talk with you about something." I walked into the sewing room. "What, Mom?" "You need to know something. Ever since you came out to us and told us you were gay, your father and I haven't been having marital relations." I was stunned by how blunt she was being. "How is that my fault?" She slid the magnifying lenses up onto her forehead so that it now seemed as though she was giving me the third-degree with two sets of eyes: "You need to straighten out, mister. You know, there's a disease associated with this now. You're going to get AIDS and all of your friends will abandon you."

She was getting more and more distraught, really working herself up as she sometimes did, and I felt like I needed to do something to calm her down. "Look, Mom, don't worry about me. I'm chaste now," I lied. "Chased? Oh, dear, no! Who's chasing you?" "No, Mom, not 'chased,' I mean 'chaste' as in chastity. I'm celibate." I thought it would throw her off her tirade, but she just got worse. "Mister, if you ever shack up with a man, you're not my son anymore."

"Bitch!" I screamed at her.

Dad burst into the room: "What's going on here?" he asked. I fled to the kitchen and sat frozen at the Formica breakfast counter, dreading what would come next. Dad caught up with me a few minutes later and said, "I understand you called your mother a bitch?" "Yeah, well did she tell you what she said to me?"

"How did this all get started?"

"I don't know, Dad, but Mom just started grilling me about me being gay for some reason, and then she really went off. I tried to calm her down by telling her that I'm celibate."

He replied, "That's good, son. You did a good thing."

And I instantly understood that he knew I was lying about being celibate, that he was telling me I had done a good thing by making up a story in order to quiet her down. We never talked directly about Mom's mental illness, how paranoid she could get, but we all had learned to do a dance with the truth to avoid any unpleasantness that might upset her. And with that—"That's good, son. You did a good thing,"—the whole incident, and the subject of my homosexuality, was swept under the rug once again. Mom and I gave each other the silent treatment for months after that, the final few months that I lived at home before moving out to finish college at SDSU.

A couple of years later my mother took her own life, and the first thing that went through my head when Dad told me over the phone, "Irene is dead; she hung herself this morning," was: "I will never have to suffer the rejection she had promised me."

Less than a year later my Dad remarried, to a good woman—Carolee—who had more experience in the world and who insisted on having everything out in the open. She wasn't going to stand for things being swept under the rug. I finally started dating for the first time in my life—was it because Mom's passing made me feel free to do so for the first time? After a failure or two, I met a guy who seemed really right for me. We dated for a year and a half, then decided to get a place together. We were so happy! But I wasn't going to play "let's pretend we're roommates," and "straighten" up our place any time my parents came to visit. So I wrote Dad and Carolee to let them know that I wanted them to come down on a Saturday to meet Marc, have some lunch, and take a walk in the park. I let them know that Marc was not just my roommate—that he was my partner. I waited nervously to see how they would respond. They accepted the invitation with apparent delight—I could tell that Carolee just couldn't wait to meet Marc—and we all got together and shared a lovely afternoon. The walk in the park was especially nice. Marc and Dad paired off. Carolee and I strolled together. "I think you've found yourself a nice fellow, there," she said. I could tell that Marc and Dad really hit it off by how much they were both smiling and laughing. I felt relieved and elated. It went so well.

But a few days later I got a letter from Dad with the 1-800 number for Homosexuals Anonymous and a statement about how they "really liked Marc and wanted to help him, too." Over the course of several weeks, Dad and I exchanged more letters. I encouraged him to read John Boswell's *Christianity, Social Tolerance, and Homosexuality*. He sent me a book I don't remember the title of, but it was basically one of those love-the-sinner-but-hate-the-sin tracts. After a bit more back-and-forth, I finally wrote to Dad. "I think this is one of those subjects where we're never going to see eye-to-eye, and we just have to accept our differences over this." Direct discussion of me being gay was swept back under the rug once again, but the evidence of it in my life was out in the open and became integrated fully into the life of my family of origin.

Marc was welcomed at the family Christmas gathering, though my oldest brother said when I told him Marc was coming, "Well, I guess you deserve to be happy, but just promise me that there won't be any public displays of affection, okay? I don't want my daughter to get confused." My niece, Lauren, actually did get a little confused when she was passing out Christmas fudge for Carolee. As Lauren approached us, I could see that she wasn't sure if she was supposed to give one package of fudge to me and one to Marc, or if she was just supposed to give one package for the two of us. Carolee saw my niece's hesitation and said, "That's okay, Lauren. Just one per family." And that seemed to instantly clear it all up, as far as my niece was concerned.

Family vacations became all-inclusive. When Marc and I planned a vacation to the Eastern Sierras that coincided with my parents' own plans to be in Mammoth, the four of us dined together frequently, and Dad and Carolee shared one of their favorite hikes with Marc and me. Dad shared with Marc about the trips his parents had taken him on to Mammoth from Los Angeles during the War in the 1940s: "We had to save our gas rations to make sure we could get up here and back." Marc told Dad about squirrel hunting in Missouri, and how his dad had told him he needed to eat the brains, "so that you can think like a squirrel." They were both clearly delighted by these conversations. A great friendship blossomed between Marc and my dad. I'm even a little jealous of it sometimes.

There have been awkward moments as well, of course. Marc and I registered our domestic partnership with the state of California in 2005. We had a ceremony, and I told everyone in the family that if they wanted an invitation, they should let me know. This invitation to receive an invitation was met with silence from Dad and from everyone else in the family. We were disappointed, but not really surprised. Three years later, when the state Supreme Court ruled in favor of marriage equality and Marc and I rushed to wed at the first opportunity, we didn't even bother letting anyone in my family know.

I've also continued to watch my dad grow in his embrace of the presence of this wonderful man in my life. He struggled at times with how to introduce Marc at the large gatherings at my brother's house that often include friends and associates from outside the family. For years, he referred to Marc simply as "our friend." Finally one year, though, as he went around introducing a large circle of family and newcomers, he came to Marc and said, in a cheery, matter-of-fact voice, "And this is Joel's partner." He told me a little later how delighted he is that I have Marc to share my life with—he just wishes we would share a life of celibacy. So he's still biblical—and still a little clinical.

A few years ago my siblings and I started talking about what to do for my dad for his eightieth birthday. We had been pooling resources to get him something swell for his major milestone birthdays. A floor jack for his seventieth, because he was still working on his own cars at that age. A portrait of the four of us for his seventy-fifth that was a reconstruction of a studio portrait taken when we were children. For his eightieth, we decided we wanted to hire a professional photographer to do a family photo session that would capture the whole extended clan—his four children, Carolee's daughter, the grandkids and great-grandkids. It was going to be a big deal. It took some time to pull it off. There were delays because of health challenges. It was no small feat to arrange a date when everyone was available.

It was well past Dad's birthday when it all came together. As the date for the photo shoot approached, I got a call from Dad. He sounded pretty serious when I answered the phone. He called to talk about just one thing. And it was clear from the tone of his voice that it was something really important to him. "Now, Joel," he said to me, "I want to be sure that you know that Marc will be in the picture." What a gift this was to me!

It had been clear to me for quite some time that my dad regarded my husband as a member of the family, so this decision and his thoughtful desire to make sure I knew about his wishes actually didn't surprise me. But it sure made me smile.

And, you know, after all these years I'd have to say my dad is still pretty biblical. But maybe not quite so Leviticus-biblical. Maybe he has become a bit more of a fan of Ecclesiastes, Chapter 4, verses 9-11:

> Two are better than one,
> because they have a good return for their labor:
> [10]If either of them falls down,
> one can help the other up.
> But pity anyone who falls
> and has no one to help them up.
> [11]Also, if two lie down together, they will keep warm.
> But how can one keep warm alone?

Tyler King

Gemini

Outside, where the moon waits,
patient, for lovers,
      poets, and the like, to finish
      romanticizing,

I trace your record scratch veins, calloused in the cold of
spring,
      and we,
      two boys,
      outside the light of heaven or
any other place,
take turns;
      once as the cross.
once as the criminal

And I awake
into two decades of dreaming,
the place where your wrists meet your palms, sweat & shine
& the contours of an unbound summer,
and sometimes
I wish
we'd have braided our hair together

and been planted like seeds into forgiving earth,
for some runaway future to uncover.

Now every night we end up
   Here;
Flipping a coin against the blood of the
covenant, to decide,
which one of us
gets to walk back through the door,
and which one has to float
   through the wall

And every night, when it lands
I kiss the letters of your name
into untorn sky, and I curse myself of
all this useless luck.

Joyce Wisdom

Baby Orchid
Is A Lesbian

It was the summer of 1967. I was fifteen. There I was in my mother's house, which used to be my grandmother's house. The house was built in an old St. Louis neighborhood that was once called Little Luxembourg. Grandma died in her bedroom in this home when I was eight.

Mother was fifty-one and always at work in her beauty salon. Her beauty salon was connected to our home, and it had its own entrance in front. But instead of using that, her customers preferred to park in back and enter the back door opening into *my* bedroom. Then they walked through the house to the salon. As a result, though it was summer, I always had to be up early, have my room clean, and bed made!

And Wednesdays! The day mom did most of her permanents! They made the whole house stink!

I bemoaned the lack of privacy in our home and I sure did not like the smells of the permanents, but I was proud of my mother.

She was born with birth defects that resulted in her missing one or even two phalanges from all her middle fingers.

Regardless, she went to beauty school after eighth grade. The school thought she would not succeed, but my grandma forced them to give her a chance. Mom graduated first in her class.

Despite the intrusions on my personal privacy, I liked the hustle and bustle of having mom's customers and friends around all the time. I learned a lot from those women. It was like having a multitude of mothers. They gave me advice, and they celebrated my successes, like: "Do Friday's homesvork Friday nighk." "Soon you vill getch your driver's permitch." "Heard your team's 10/2 for da season." "You shuld be a teacher."

Mrs. Hartman reminded me repeatedly, "Vhen you vere born, the Lemay Community Link paper published a schtory vit da headline, *Baaby Orchid is Born!*"

This was because Mom's salon was called the Orchid Beauty Salon. The clipping is still in mom's scrapbook.

However, Mom and I had been fighting a lot in 1967. It usually went this way: "No! I am never going to take over the beauty salon! Yes! I am going *away* to college!" Mom was going through menopause and I was going through adolescence. There were hormones bouncing everywhere! Mom would say, "My business vill be my legacy to you." But, like my mother and grandmother, I was strong willed. I had to stretch my own wings.

I was the first in my family to go to college. Other than my teachers, we knew almost no one who had gone before me.

I soon discovered there was another reason for my strong urge to get away. I was away at school only a short time before I fully realized I was a lesbian. It is a lot easier to come out from a distance than to come out in what might be a hostile family that you have to live with. But my family was not hostile. They said, "Vee don't exactly underschtand, but vee love you."

They had not been brainwashed by anti-gay hate. This was (and is) surprising in Missouri. I was a lucky young woman.

But on this day in 1967, there was another angst in the air. Mom was told she had breast cancer and had scheduled her mastectomy. Little did I know that I would be doing the same, just 15 years later, when I was only 30. She was not happy about that legacy she left me.

But my mom and I—we both kicked cancer's butt!!

Kelly Bowen

Tiger

I always heard stories about the "carnie people" at the Del Mar Fair. My older brother Mike and I used to go every summer. We would walk around and around the fun zone, the game operators cajoling us to come try to win their prizes. The ride operators all looked far too ill-equipped to actually make sure we were safe on the rides. Mike always talked about how I shouldn't trust the carnies: they were unsafe and unclean, diseased and absolutely nefarious. As we walked, he would point to those who were missing teeth, or workers who were particularly grimy, to reinforce why it was absolutely imperative to steer clear. They were, at best, out to steal from anyone gullible enough to fall prey to them and their rigged games. He left the worst vague, but hinted at physical harm and kidnapping because he liked watching my fear, knowing my imagination would weave horrible possibilities of forced substances, assault, maiming, and of never being able to escape. Even to associate with the carnies could somehow taint me with their foul intentions, as if they had some preternatural power of corruption.

When I was seventeen, my friend Steve's band got a gig at the fair. This was a big deal in high school! At the time, my friend group consisted of me—the lone girl—and nine fairly mismatched guys. I used to make jokes about my having all-male friends to hide the oddity of the situation from myself. One of the guys was Ed, my best friend at the time. We'd gotten super close, and I thought I could depend on him for anything. Ed and I, as well as two of the other guys, made plans to go to the concert together to support and celebrate our buddy. Steve and I had dated for a few months. Though it had been a while since we'd broken up, I was still infatuated, and thus was desperately trying to nurse along a friendship to retain what little I could of him. There was no way I was going to miss his show.

We got there early, not wanting to risk being late. Unknown to all of our young minds, playing at the fair didn't exactly mean you'd have a big crowd. Steve's band was booked on one of the smaller stages, with bleachers set up flat in front of it. We walked up to practically empty seating, with just a smattering of tired fair-goers sitting towards the back, using the bleachers to rest their feet. Undaunted, we walked forward, and sat in the fourth row, so that Steve would be right in front of us. The benches ahead of us were empty.

Steve and his band came out and started playing. We cheered with excessive enthusiasm. I was immediately absorbed in their set, and so proud of my friend.

Then, a disheveled figure walked out from behind stage right, limping, and looking quite dirty. The movement caught my attention, and the oddity kept it. It took me a moment to realize it was a woman, only really discernable by her overall petite stature and build, and by my gut instinct, as she was clothed in nondescript jeans and the same shirt all the carnies wore. Even at the distance I was from her, there was something alarming about her appearance. She paused alongside the stage, and did a quick scan of the sparse crowd. Her eyes landed on me like a homing beacon. And then she moved again.

She limped forward, alongside the stage, eyes locked on me the whole time. She passed across the front of the stage, until she was on the outside aisle nearest me. Still hobbling, she came up the aisle.

As she neared, I saw she was not much older than I was. There was a crooked gash across her forehead that was clearly recently scabbed and barely healed. Her bangs were hacked jaggedly as if cut by a toddler.

She paused for a moment at our row, but then moved past to the one behind where I sat with my friends. She sauntered in and plopped herself down on the bench right behind me. She leaned forward, legs spread wide in a masculine stance, and started talking in my ear.

"Hi, I'm Melissa," she declared in an overly dramatically low voice, to my immobilized self. "But my friends call me Tiger."

She extended her left arm to shake my hand. I was taught to be polite, so while completely confused, I extended my left hand in response. As she reached for my hand, she showed me her right. Hand held straight from her arm, her wrist extended down several inches at an alarming angle. She went on to explain that she'd been in a motorcycle accident the week prior. She'd broken her wrist, but decided the cast was a drag, and had taken it off. The limp and the gash were also from the accident.

I was suddenly desperate with alarm, and clueless as to what to do. All of my brother's stories about the carnies reared up in my mind, and now one had me in her sights. I'd just shaken her hand too! I wanted to run, but then I'd be leaving Steve's show and my friends.

She asked rhetorically, "So, I see you're here with the guys."

"Yes," I replied, not understanding. "I'm here with my friends."

"So, they're all *guys*," she pressed. "*Just* guys." She leaned further forward, a gleam in her eye. "Does that mean you do *everything* guys do?"

Now, at a mere seventeen, I'd had a boyfriend or two. I'd also had a girlfriend, though I was utterly conflicted about that and in complete denial about my sexuality. I was a pretty shy teen, not willing to step forward and stand up for myself. I just wanted to watch Steve and the damned band! She was stealing my precious moments with him.

I responded by only muttering, "Yes they're my friends, and I don't really know what you mean." Hoping she'd take the hint, I turned back to the stage.

She leaned forward further. The motion demanded I look at her again. "What I *mean* is, do you like women? Like, *sexually* like women?"

I panicked. She was terrifying! Dirty, and injured and deranged enough to have removed a cast! Clearly she would do anything to get what she wanted. My friends didn't know I had slept with a woman. I had never intended what had happened with Julie, my former best friend who then became that girlfriend. We had just found ourselves crossing that line. All I knew was that as much as kissing her, touching her, and being touched by her was exhilarating, it was also shameful and forbidden, and somehow that made me lesser, or bad. Young and thoroughly confused, after we'd ceased our romantic involvement, I had compartmentalized those experiences away in a desperate desire to fit in.

"No! No, I don't like *women*!" I stammered, as if she were daft. "Gosh, these are just my friends!" I wasn't helping my case in the least. My words only further decried the realities I denied, but which somehow, even this carnie girl could see.

Tiger persisted. She was relentless. "Well, you haven't really lived until you've tried everything. You really should. You'd be surprised at what you might learn."

It finally dawned on me: she was hitting on me! I'd never been hit on by a woman before, and I was deeply unnerved. Even if she hadn't been a carnie, there was nothing remotely attractive about Tiger. Her words caused my past romance with Julie to flash through my mind, replete with details of what we'd tried, how it felt, and all of my confusion. My sense of shame roared to life.

At this point, I gave Ed a look. I was desperate for someone, *anyone*, to save me. He shrugged and looked at me with a "What the fuck am I supposed to do?" in his eyes and went back to watching the band. He hadn't paid me or Tiger any heed, and if he'd heard a word she said, he didn't care.

I was horrified. My best friend had failed me. I was on my own. I could barely think. All the stories my brother told me ran through my head in rapid succession. If I was rude, she'd go back to "her people" and they'd come hurt me, and come hurt my friends. I imagined a horde of large, muscled carnies beating us bloody for my transgression.

With my mind, I tried to will Ed into putting an arm around me, to pretend, even for five seconds, to be a boyfriend. My panic-stricken eyes beamed at him. He kept his face turned towards the stage, reinforcing my aloneness.

Tiger took this all in, and brazenly forged ahead. "I've tried a lot of things. There's really way more to life than you've seen. You haven't lived until you've made love to a woman. It's amazing."

I sputtered inconsequentially, trying to shut her down, "I've lived… I've, I've… lived… p… p… *plenty!*" My mind was frozen between my fear of her and the realities of my past. That was the best I could come up with. I feebly added, "I have! Lots!" I was as ineffective in convincing her to leave as I had been in getting Ed to save me. I slumped in my seat, wanting to melt into its metal until there was nothing left of me for her to see.

With a devilish look in her eyes and a wry grin on her lips, she said, "You should come to the carnie party tonight. It'll be amazing. You have a car, right?"

Stupid me, I nodded, because I did have a car, and who was I to lie, even to protect myself.

I sat there, half-facing the stage, half-facing Tiger, like a lump on the bench. I was afraid to turn away from her, rooted in place. I wanted to run, wanted to hide, wanted to be anywhere but there. The only problem was: I was there to see Steve's band, I was there with my friends, and I was Ed's ride. I couldn't leave. Where would I go, alone, during the set? Assuredly, Tiger would follow me.

I shut down, unable to walk away, mired in place by the life I'd been bred to live and by the shame I'd tried to bury.

She persisted through the rest of the show. Wheedling me. Telling me how much of life I was missing out on not being with women. How amazing the party would be. I could come just for a bit. Then I'd see how it was, and would know I'd made the right choice.

The entirety of Steve's gig past the third song faded into the background and became a blur. My excitement was entirely burned away by my fear and my abject inability to get her to leave. I was frantic with my need to escape.

When the set ended, miraculously, she just got up and left, but I was still terrified. I was absolutely convinced she was watching me from the shadows, watching us. That she would follow us for the night, and accost me at my car, pleading for a ride, and for me to go to the party with her. I was sure she would have a bunch of even scarier carnie people in tow, to make sure we complied. I was convinced I wasn't safe. I couldn't get out of the fair fast enough.

I didn't attend the fair for several decades after that night. It took my marriage to get me back. My failed marriage, in which as my husband and I splintered apart, I'd let myself be swooped up by a woman, even then still fighting my deepest longings. Our only day at the fair was one last painful family outing, intended to give our daughter the memory of fun and rides while accompanied by both of her parents. Desire to bring my daughter joy spearheaded me onto the path of facing long held fears and letting them go.

The carnie girl turned out to be right. Eventually, years after my marriage ended, I came to realize truly, it's women I am most innately attracted to, and that my life is much fuller and complete with a woman in it, but not because of the sex alone. It's the connection, the bonding, and being true to my heart.

Tiger was frightening. In many ways, she encapsulated what I feared my sexuality meant. That I, too, was dirty and disturbing, and would be viewed as a deviant not welcome in society. That my friends wouldn't help me made me feel alone and like I'd already been shunned, causing me to push it further down in my psyche.

I can still hear the breathy, artificially low-pitched intonation of her voice in my mind as she said, "Hi, I'm Melissa, but my friends call me Tiger."

It took years for me to accept myself as I am, and to understand and finally feel that my sexuality isn't shameful and doesn't mark me as inherently repulsive. I wish I'd had the self confidence Tiger had then, and that I have now. The comfort in my own skin. The ability to set boundaries and to choose who I want in my world. To have simply shut her down with, "Hi, Melissa."

Edward Elliott

Freshly Baked Bread

It starts as a small feeling. Quiet in nature, almost as though you could ignore it and it would simply fade away like breath-fogged glass. A soft incongruence. Something you don't even see unless you reach for it, making you wonder if you weren't just making it all up. But occasionally, the raw nerves would catch an edge and you would see clearly for just one second, before it all evaporated into the mist.

Mild frustration, like when your brother got a blue Chinese lantern in his Easter basket, and you got a pink one, and it *just isn't fair*, because you wanted a blue one too, and this pink one makes you feel strange in a way you don't quite have the words to describe yet. But you suppose it's alright. After all, you're a girl and he's a boy, and it's only the way things work.

Sometimes it's just a lacy bit of nothing, like when you put on your first bra and look in the mirror, and all you see is your grandmother's blouse and someone you don't really recognize. She looks like you, but you're not even sure *you* look like you. You're not even sure who that is. You realize that every bit of yourself that you know was stolen from somewhere else. Your clothes were stolen from the 1960s comics you got at the store by the beach, trying to imitate a girl you can only see if you twist your head all the way around and stare until the world is just bits of shapes and color. Your sense of self is gone.

What shred of identity you had was stolen from yourself, or at least a concept of yourself you thought you could see glimpses of when you looked at the reflection in your friends' pupils. You're no longer sure the person you thought you were ever really existed. At night, you dream of cobbled city streets and homemade bread, shops and horse races and people you don't know, like the ones in your American Girl mystery books and the ones you can sometimes see for an instant if you hear the right note. Memories so old you're not even sure they're yours cling to the edges of your subconscious, activated only when you feel truly alone, only when you move slowly enough to feel a different air on your skin, chilling and comforting. Some nights, you lay in bed grasping at every thread you can remember, trying to weave them into a complete picture. You're not sure how much is real, but It's a nice distraction from a very real identity crisis looming on the horizon. A simpler place lives behind your mind. One full of warm, comforting bread and things that make more sense. You close your eyes every chance you get, imagining a whole world stretched out before you. Clocks reset, the right clothes on your back, and a completely new identity to design. But when you open your eyes, the girl in the mirror is still staring back at you. You suppose you might enjoy getting to know her if she stuck around for a while. At least that's what your mother says. Puberty is just a difficult time.

Sometimes it was just confusion, like at your girls' support group in 8th grade during the exercise where everyone steps forward to share things that happened to them to prove that no one is alone in their struggles. It was actually a really nice activity, and many girls found solace in the sense of female community. You see this community, and you want to be a part of it. Perhaps dreams of bread were only a fantasy. Around you is tangible companionship. So you step forward to confess that you wish you were a boy sometimes, and not *a single other girl* steps forward, so you stand there, with your messy pixie cut and oversized button up wondering where it all went wrong.

At some point, The Feeling went from a whisper of an idea to a sticky membrane coating your entire body. It was thin enough that you could almost forget it was there, but thick enough that you had a breakdown in the bathroom at the park because you couldn't get your makeshift binder tight enough to stop the bleeding emotions flowing from the open wounds on your face. Nothing was tight enough to armor your insides against the onslaught of deep puncture wounds, sharp pain that felt like someone or something was trying to knife its way out of you like a hunter dissecting a deer, opening your ribcage like a flower at dawn.

You look things up one day, and find out the name for your pain: *Gender Dysphoria.* There are other people like you. There are other people feeling the same things. You feel comforted and terrified all at once. Ahead of you stretches a back-breaking journey that you don't want to take. If only you could remove the bits of you that are causing so much pain. If only you could rip out the tangled roots of mistaken identity and make your body a home. You let your tears fall in the car one day, and your mother doesn't understand. After all, what kind of terrible parent would support her own daughter to cut up her body? For the first time in your life you feel like a stranger, unsafe and insecure in your own home. For the first time in your life, you wonder if you can be trusted with the control of your own life. You wonder if anyone else can be either.

The day you got your first real binder was one of total relief. The Feeling slipped back into the darkness for just one night. Your one solace, the LGBT youth center, dishing out visions of a brighter future like plates of Costco cake at a Skate World birthday party. Fluorescent rainbow dreams that were so close, but you were grasping at thin air, fingers just brushing the corner of paradise, until you leapt out of the closet like a fish jumping at last into a pristine lake, grabbing a mouthful of fresh bread on the way down. You finally caught the edge of a pride float and The Feeling melted away for an afternoon.

Then back to the real world, and it wasn't as different as you'd hoped. The lake turned out to be another, slightly bigger bowl. Halls full of people only half-trying to humor you. The viscous membrane was back, no longer able to be ignored. New tendrils appeared, burrowing inward like flesh knives ready to carve you all apart into oozing blobs of flesh chunks and slime. Even the sovereign world behind your eyes turned sour. What was once exciting and full of opportunity is now terrifying and claustrophobic. You feel phantom wounds on your skin that mirror the seams from which your sense of self falls apart.

You kept your ribs together fairly well, with more and more elaborate clothing routines, layers upon layers of shirts and jackets, like the layers and layers of dysphoria painted on your body like a second skin. One you wish you could cut yourself out of, like the knives cleaving your flesh into bite-size pieces. Maybe it would be worth the effort to take out all of the organs. Or maybe there was a zipper somewhere? There wasn't. Just you and your skin suit that was just a little bit too loose, and a little bit too tight in all the wrong places. You yell at your father one day, demanding that he acknowledge the person you're becoming. Just a few words, but you wish you could say more. You wish you could be quieter, and you wish you knew how to be loud. You wish you could articulate the horrible misshapen bits of yourself that he never understood existed. But life continued, and you never spoke about it again.

Calendar boxes stacked the days together in sets of five, but they all stuck around you in clumps. You grabbed the edges to pull them off but they only ended up smearing together in a long chain, no longer recognizable as separate entities. Every minute felt like swimming in melted glass. The truth was on the tip of your tongue, and the cure was on the shelf next to you, but your voice didn't work and your hands were tied down. Fridays filled with pizza and the comfort of queer camaraderie broke up the monotony. Loneliness is harder to bear when you're being eaten up from the inside out. Blurred months dampened moments. The second skin acted as just another shield around your mind, covering up any trace of human thoughts and feelings, saving your mental playground for you and only you. In your dreams at night, you run and fight for every scrap of bread.

It wasn't all bad, though. By the end of the year you were learning to cope. Solace emerged, and your second Pride was caught up in a whirlwind of new people, new experiences, and colorful new feelings, ones you almost felt safe enough to let fall from the enclosure you had created in your head. Almost. Good things sometimes sour before you can even tell. Good times sometimes only look that way through the unconscious lens of guilt. Rainbows and sweet nighttime talks quickly revealed frantic calls and accusations, struggling to breathe at every electronic buzz. Absolutes of judgement squeezed at your heart and lungs, threatening to smash them flat and roll them out into a soft blanket for you to give as a birthday gift. Confusion and guilt clouded every action and memory. You cared too much and not enough at the same time.

But, as all things do, that ended. You fell back to your close friends and tried to forget, remembering why friends were there to begin with. Closer bonds formed, and good memories wallpapered over the old. Homemade fresh bread tasted better than you ever imagined. Finally, finally, the gate was lifted and you tasted the flavor of triumph. The Feeling melted away as you sanded down the soft edges of your meat suit. Sun poked through the clouds, and the scent of fresh baked bread filled the hallways of your dreams, awakening your senses to thousands of possibilities you'd never considered.

Oh, my dear, dear man. I wish I could save you from every time you fought with your parents, from every time your identity melted down your body like soft cheese in the sun. From every time you felt like you would never be home anywhere. From every time the weight of this burden crushed the emotion out of you like a Styrofoam cup at the bottom of the ocean.

But it will be gone sooner than you think. It's not perfect yet, and it may never be. But it will be close enough, a little closer every moment we choose. Someday, The Feeling will be back to the whisper it once was, and one day, one day in the future, we will sit in a comfortable chair and feel the gentle weight of two perfectly tailored suits, and we will realize that we haven't felt that feeling in quite a while. We will look for the incongruence and try again to remember what it felt like to be in the wrong skin. The secret world in the back of our mind will no longer be needed, and it will fade away into the obscurity of history, as it was always meant to. We will look for The Feeling and find that the space it once occupied has been filled with fresh bread, warm, just the way we like it.

And we will be together, and we will be content.

Jasz Kuyaté Cabrera

Them

Hi, my name's (redacted) and
my pronouns are
not taken seriously.
You look at me curiously, but
you're not the only ones
I've furiously pleaded to

Pleaded for equality, greeted to
excuses so low quality, I can count the pixels.

One.
How can you use those pronouns,
but you're only a singular person?
Two.
That's too hard for me. Why can't you just use normal
pronouns?
Three.
There's only two genders dipshit.

One.
Nobody ever notices their own use of they/them
until it's requested of them.

My demand brings reprimand, my request banned and I'm told to man
up.

Two.

Too hard for you? Too hard to remove the shiv in my side that YOU are holding in place?
The blade I've taken to my own flesh to sculpt it to match in the mirror what I see in my heart.

Three.

There's never only been two genders. Shit, there's never even been only two sets of equipment.
This eurocentric, christian-centric culture, can't handle my eccentric identity.
See it's only ever the cis white shark, clinging desperately to Reagan's empire that holds me and my enby siblings down.

The two spirit natives of the American continent, thrived in their community
but stripped of dignity when your values were made superior.

The muxe in Mexico. Born like me, look like me, live like me in ambiguity

The hijra/Aravani/Aruvani/Jagappa predominantly of South Asia. An official third gender recognized in India.
Seen as neither wholly male or female.

The samoan fa'afafine. Much like the muxe. Born like me, look like me, at birth assigned male.
Like me.
But they embody full masc and femininity.

The glorious Indonesian people
recognize five genders in Bugis society
makkunrai, oroané, bissu, calabai, and calalai
Makkunrai for the cisgender guy
Oroané is cis, but the other way.
Calabai and Calalai a trans man or woman's alibi
and the bissu are commonly called gender transcendent
transcendent of such strict binary rules
yet all five genders live in harmony

The unique galli. Self castrating priests of Cybele. Begging
the question, does one lose their entire identity if
they lose what's in their pants?

The two-spirits, the muxe, the hijra, the fa'afafine, calalai,
calabai, bissu, the onnagata, the kathoey, the
mukhanna, the fatada, the pavaya, the khasua, the khoja,
the jogappa, the ali, the basir, the manang, and the cults
of Inanna, Ishtar, Cybele, Astargatis, Bahucharā Mātā,
Yellamma and Chatushsrngi, all the AFAB men in fields of
study wearing trousers 30 years to be seen as an equal buddy.
I count 24 and you're stuck on 2
I was approached at a music festival once
A couple hot summers ago, before my hair started to flow
Yes it was my fault I was in Arizona, I know
But I just had to get that $35 ticket to see P!@tD

He was eyeing me all day before he broke silence and asked
me my name
(redacted)—I said with hopeful naivety
but somehow that wasn't the right answer
Is that your real name? Is that on your ID?

Yes—I said but all he saw was my hesitation
and somehow that wasn't the right answer
With a venomous look he pressed on
Are you really a girl? His eyes glaring through my Fall Out
Boy bandana around my throat as if glancing at a growth
of cartilage in my trachea would provide evidence for his
answer
Yes—I said, but somehow that wasn't the right answer
Well, whatchu got in your pants? He dared ask
So I reached down and pulled out my knife
And somehow that wasn't the right answer

Now, this is just a pocket comb to tame my wild hair
But why do I have a brush with death every time I'm
genuine, it isn't fair
Why does a threat lurk when I step out my door
When I'm bothering no one else
When all I want to do is express acceptance of myself
and to take my partner's hand
without fear of someone taking my head.

Hi, my name is (redacted) and my
pronouns are not he/him
Don't try to force me, it doesn't fit
It used to fit
It kinda fit
Like wearing a pair of boxer shorts backwards
It's "supposed" to fit and it gets the job done
and it was built for these parts
but it doesn't fit
It's uncomfortable and makes me feel
gross
I get to choose what to wear

My pronouns are not he/him
because my masculinity is not fragile
I'm not afraid to cry, only to raise my voice
I'm aware of how much space I take up
I don't make excuses when my actions make someone
uncomfortable
I apologize, I listen, I learn
I don't use my anger to get my way
I don't force my way
especially when I'm wrong

Hi, my name's (redacted) and my
pronouns are not he/him
and they're not she/her.
I don't attract the male gaze (that's g-a-z-e), I benefit off
inherent misogyny
I've never been called out on my resting bitch face
I don't get talked over
I don't feel comfortable buying clothes
I don't feel comfortable buying clothes that would make me
feel comfortable
I'm afraid every time I walk down a feminine aisle in Target
I'm afraid every time I dress, the last time I wore this I had
to run to Arizona.

I've seen sideways glances and more disgust aimed at me
for wearing a dress or
for explaining that the first tattoo I got is my pride flag for
genderqueer
I get more rejection explaining what the purple and green
represent
than I do explaining how I got my scars.

It took 21 years for me to realize
that I was lactose intolerant
21 years is too long to learn that your body
will never accept something you
keep shoving into it

At 5, I experienced painful stomach aches
At 9, I quit during soccer practice
because the gas in my stomach
made it so I couldn't breathe
In my adolescence, I read that 7 farts a day
was normal, and I was hitting 7 an an hour

So, I learned to hide it, hold it, and only
release it when it I was alone
My very existence was this uncomfortable
tension of poisoning my body with the very thing the
majority of people digested easily

At 21 I realized that milk poisoned my body
It took me another year to start to accept I was trans.

Hi, my name's (redacted) and my
pronouns are they/them/theirs.
Learn it.

Kelsey Schultz

Honey

As a sheltered, lonely kid growing up without close friends, I didn't learn how to build relationships and be myself until college and grad school. There, I found my people in the weirdos who felt invisible or didn't "fit in". As an adult, I'm pretty proud of my community and the bold, intuitive, sassy woman I've become.

But, it's hard to shrug off those aching years of longing to connect. I'm still afraid of hurting others, and I often feel indebted to people who express romantic or sexual interest in me. Asking for what I need is foreign to me. It feels selfish, especially when someone has already offered me time, commitment, and love.

That came to a head when I was twenty-seven and met Drew, the first person I dated who made *sense* to me. Then Drew led me to Mary, who *also* made sense to me.

It all started when I spilled my guts on the Diversionary Theater's stage in San Diego, telling one of my most vulnerable stories to an audience full of strangers.

A day after the performance, I received an email from someone who was there - Drew. We'd met at a few storytelling events and shows in the last couple years, but never really talked. Boldly complimenting my performance, he wrote things like, "You offered a vulnerability that the audience immediately recognized as truth," "you use your face like an instrument, and to great effect," and "I hope you felt the standing ovation you earned, even if you couldn't see it." At the bottom, he asked "Would you like to get drinks sometime?" and included 3 check boxes - yes, no thank you, and there are important things to communicate before I can answer this responsibly. How could I resist a writer like *that*?!

On our first date, up close and personal, Drew's intensity translated to his physical presence. He stood at over six feet, dressed in a chic black outfit, filling the restaurant's door frame with a burly chest and thick arms adorned with dark tattoos. You could feel his stormy energy enter the room. We talked as if we were old friends, digging into our dating history, fears, and dreams. I couldn't stop staring at his sharp jawline and striking blue eyes.

Late in the evening, he reached across the table to cup my hands in his. Leveling me with his gaze, he asked, "So, what'd you think of my email?" Leaving the restaurant, we made out on the hood of my car, oblivious to passerby. We just clicked. On *all* the levels. Normally, I was the one to put on the brakes, but my body knew before my mind did. By our *third date,* we both said I love you and meant it. He even joined my trip to Colorado a month later, the state I dreamed of moving to, so he could explore living there in the future.

Drew wanted to introduce me to more people in his life. With a few of his friends, we went out to a dive bar. Sidling up to the bartender to order drinks, they started bellowing loudly at a short woman at the other side of the room. "MARYYYY!"

She slowly turned; tight blond curls in a cropped page boy haircut. Jean jacket. Grandpa glasses. Rounded off with thick, black combat boots.

I felt like I was on an episode of Butch Baywatch.

As she walked over to our rowdy group, my knees melted. A small, gorgeous smile spread across her face when she reached us. She said, "Are you Kelsey?" I thought she must've been mistaken. *How could this sexy masculine pixie know my name?* "I've heard so much about you! I'm Mary, Drew's roommate."

Fuck.

Mary and I quickly bonded, swapping stories about bad breakups over a glass of wine. She lamented a girlfriend who left her heartbroken a year prior. I was hypnotized by her raw grief and our instant connection. I'd had an unrequited crush on a woman and another on a non-binary friend before, and plenty of queer celebrities like Ruby Rose or Natalie Morales. Did that mean I was gay? Or... gay enough for Mary? I mean, I drive a Subaru. I love my Birkenstocks. I had an edgy, asymmetrical haircut. Almost all of my closest friends fell somewhere on the queer spectrum, and they wouldn't be surprised.

Here I was, at twenty-seven, still full of questions and no clue of how to start answering them without hurting anyone. It wasn't like these ideas had *never* crossed my mind, I just never had a real opportunity to act on them. Mary made me want to act.

Even so, what if I was too queer for Drew? He wasn't the type to have a lesbian fantasy, not that I wanted him to. I wasn't sure how far I was willing to go to answer my longing. Could I be in separate relationships with Mary and Drew at the same time? Who did I think I was?!? My high school self wouldn't have recognized me. I could imagine how my boomer parents happily married for over thirty years would recoil or roll their eyes at the idea of this "poly-whosie-what millennial bullshit," even if they would probably try to accept my attraction to multiple genders.

All of this felt self-serving and complicated, so I tried to ignore my crush on her at first. It started innocently enough, but the more time I spent with Drew, the more time I spent with Mary.

One time, Mary and I were hanging out at a bar, waiting for Drew to come. She started opening up when I peppered her with questions before she shyly changed the subject, like she always did. She asked if I'd ever heard of Andrea Gibson, one of my favorite slam poets. Excitedly, I told her I knew "*Honey*," one of their most epic love poems ever written, by heart. "Prove it!" she grinned, and pressed play on her phone. My heart pounded in my chest. Locking eyes with Mary, I recited the poem line by line. The air crackled with energy as we leaned in closer and closer, the room melting away.

Drew showed up, joined by a mutual friend, who whipped her head back and forth between Mary and me. She turned to Drew and joked, "Are we interrupting? Do you two need a room?" As Drew obliviously chuckled, Mary and I broke eye contact. The magic disintegrated into thin air.

Another night, Mary slayed a storytelling performance. Aching with vulnerability, I watched her glow with courage as she unapologetically laid her truth bare at the podium. Rushing off stage afterwards, she snuck up behind me and *sunk her teeth* into my *shoulder*. "What'd you think?" she whispered in my ear. Goosebumps shot down my body as I turned to respond, but she silenced me as she gently pressed some bread into my mouth. Chewing, I laughed at her audacity while she grinned and winked, leaning toward me again with another piece of her roll. Drew was distracted talking with friends and carrying on—it was our little world again. Mary *knew* what she was doing. It took everything in me not to close the gap and tension between us, though I couldn't stop images of her haunting my dreams after that.

Things were going really well with Drew, who didn't seem to notice anything out of the ordinary. Actually, we openly talked about polyamory, asking each other questions like "do you think it would hurt more if your partner loved someone else or had sex with someone else?" and "is there a finite amount that you can love another person?" Though theoretical, these conversations invited a radical level of honesty and trust neither of us experienced before. We didn't pretend to have any answers, only feeling safe enough to express genuine curiosity and share an intellect and connection I fell for in the first place.

Theory was fine, but this was his roommate. Here I was, barging into their home and fucking up their lives. This might be for nothing—I could just be some bicurious straight girl leading on a very queer woman, or making up all this chemistry in my head. Having a crush was hard enough. I didn't believe anyone in their right mind would think I was worth it, or ever agree to a complicated mess even I struggled to explain. I decided to trust myself to know when it was the right time to say anything, so I waited.

One weekend, a couple months after Mary and I met, Drew had a camping trip with some friends and I already had work plans, so I couldn't go. Packing his bags, he said, "Hey, I'm kind of worried about Mary. She's been super hermit-y lately. Can you check on her? You seem to bring her out of her shell."

I'm almost embarrassed by how eagerly I texted Mary; as luck would have it, she had 2 tickets to a Maggie Rogers concert, and no one to go with her! That night at the concert, our bodies shimmered with sweat and alcohol, at one with the mass swaying to the glory that *is* Maggie Rogers. We moved closer and closer, brushing against each other with flirty abandon. Drunk, steam floating off our hot skin, we stood on the curb outside of The Observatory, talking—my favorite thing to do with her.

I told Mary about my intention to move to Colorado. She slipped her hand into mine and said off-handedly, "Boulder is stunning. I would totally live there, kid." As she stared into my eyes, I saw the green light I'd been waiting for. She could see herself in Colorado? It wasn't just me—she was into this! It didn't matter what I was anymore—queer? Polyamorous? Whatever, I knew I was into Mary. Bonus: there was a possibility of a future. This was enough, it was real, and I had to explore us. The cologne on her jacket smelled like aftershave. Wafts of it pulled me toward her, desire pulsing through me. Her warm, expectant mouth was inches from mine, but I couldn't. This wasn't a stranger, this was my partner's roommate and friend. I needed a permission slip from Drew if I was going through with this. It took lady balls of steel for me to not follow Mary home that night.

Buzzing with sexual tension and unexpressed emotion that evening, I tried to call Drew until I remembered he was camping with no cell service. Opening my laptop, I poured my guts into an eloquent 991-word letter. I dared to ask for the impossible: telling Drew that I loved him *and* I couldn't betray myself by not exploring this, even if it meant he would leave me.

My impatience got the better of me—I heard my inbox ding to confirm it was sent. At that moment, I realized I'd *come out as queer* and told my boyfriend I had feelings for *his roommate* in an *email*. Swallowing the vomit creeping up the back of my throat, I forwarded the message to three of my most supportive LGBTQ+ friends and asked for guidance. With their reassurance and love, I was able to wait for Drew to contact me.

Later the next day, Drew texted me a cheerful, "Hey, boo! I'm back and have a ton of work emails to sift through, so I'll be quiet tonight. Love you!" with a little smiley face.

I felt the blood drain from my face. "Haha, sounds great!" I replied. "So glad you're back! Did you already read the email from me?" trying my best to stay calm and casual. Little bubbles appeared on my screen: "I didn't see one... Oh wait, there it is!" A few seconds passed, more bubbles, then: "Oh. *Oh.*"

Seized by a full-on panic attack, fingers slick with sweat, I rapid-fire texted:

"DO NOT OPEN IT, DEAR GOD. DAMN MY IMPATIENCE".

"WAIT, NO! READ IT, IT'S OK, I'M FINE!"

"GOING TO FRIEND'S HOUSE. NEED HER AND DOGS. NOT FINE BUT WILL BE IN GOOD HANDS."

"Did I mention I love you? Because I really do, I swear!!"

"I'm SO sorry I didn't ask, how was your camping trip?! God, and you must be exhausted, I'm so sorry. This is crazy and selfish."

I snagged my keys and ran across the street to my best friend's place, one I'd forwarded the email to the night before. Hot, terrified tears burned down my cheeks as I heaved on the sidewalk outside her apartment. My phone chirped and buzzed in my pocket; Drew had responded. "Honey, what is going on? Do you want me to come over? It's okay if you want me to wait! I love you, too. I missed you all weekend, I thought about you the whole time."

Sitting on the grassy curb, I put my head between my legs, letting my breath become heavy and slow. Picking up my phone, I replied, "Hi. Thank you for being so sweet and calm. I'm doing a lot better, just had a much stronger reaction than expected which is why I wrote that email in the first place.

Could you read it, then we can talk about it tomorrow? And if you need to talk sooner, you can let me know?"

Without missing a beat, Drew replied, "Absolutely, of course. Get some rest."

After crying about it with my friend, a sleepless night followed by a long work day, I realized I was ramping up the pressure on myself, not Drew, who'd always responded with grace. Anxiously, I had no idea what to expect when I walked into his house the next evening. Mercifully, Mary was out.

What if he wasn't okay with it? How much was I willing to give up? We sat on his bed, facing each other. Taking a deep breath, I said, "So, since you read my letter, you know that I'm queer and have feelings for Mary. I think she has feelings for me, too. *And I love you.*"

Nodding, Drew cleared his throat. "Yeah, and I'm glad you're okay. You know I'm open to the idea of polyamory. I wouldn't have been upset if something had happened this weekend." That didn't surprise me, given our previous conversations. Admittedly, I felt a small ache of regret for not going for it when I had the chance with Mary, though I'm not sure I would've been able to forgive myself if I had.

Quickly jumping in, I said, "Thank you for that. I couldn't ignore this anymore. I have to explore it. So, I want to see if we can find a way to honor what we have and respect your relationship with Mary, too. I'm going to shut up now."

Drew sighed, straightened his back, then gave me a firm, hard stare. "I'm going to need more time to think about it, but for now, here's what I know: first, I love you and both of you deserve to be happy. Also, I have two conditions: One: tell me when it happens. I don't need details, I just don't want to be left in the dark. Two, no talking about me when you're together. Sound fair?"

It was a bit of a curt listicle, but I was honored he could give me that much. Oddly, the growing tension I'd felt to connect with Mary was so much lighter, knowing I would still be loved by this incredible person. When Drew and I were talking about my romantic feelings for someone else, the last thing I expected to feel was a deeper connection with him. This wasn't going to be easy, but for the first time, I felt a glimmer of hope—could I ask for what I wanted and everything wouldn't fall apart? No matter what happened with Mary, I knew I'd found a partner who would always have my back.

That night, I wrote another epic letter, this time, to Mary. In two-and-a-half pages and 1489 words, I laid out what I had to offer, and what I wanted. To spend more time with her, and to know if she felt the same attraction I did. I told her to take the time she needed, and sent the email.

I didn't expect her to need *two weeks*. Yeah, *two weeks later*, she finally responded at about one in the morning. The first line of her message was "I'm really drunk and high right now," and read like bad poetry as she detailed how her life was a mess, she hadn't healed yet from her ex who broke up with her a year prior, and she wasn't interested in polyamory. Mary made the choice for me.

Reading the letter over and over, I thought I was fine. *I already have a partner, whatever. It's not like she really mattered, or like I thought this would work anyway.* Then I started shaking with sobs.

Despite all those moments with Mary, risking everything with a panicked confession to my partner, writing a freakin' love letter, and still only in the wake of rejection did it feel real. My body knew before I did. This mattered. Mary was more than a friend to me, and this sucked.

After a few more messages back and forth, we wished each other well. Unrelated to the letter, she packed up her life a few weeks later, and decided to travel and live out of her truck. I haven't heard from her since.

I wasn't wrong for wanting Mary, or for being hurt by the way she responded. Although she was no longer in our lives physically, polyamory was something Drew and I considered. We never had the opportunity and I didn't have the desire to act upon it.

Claiming space in a relationship and asking for what I wanted is what changed everything, not being queer or polyamorous. A year later, I took the next perfect job offer and followed my dream of moving to Colorado. Choosing to end my relationship with Drew because it couldn't meet my needs was one of the hardest decisions I ever made, especially given his incredible support and our connection through that time. It's hard to imagine a better cis-male partner for me to have gone through that chapter of my queer story with. Although we weren't strong enough to survive my choice to move, I will always love Drew for setting a strong precedent for any future partners that I could trust by my side—regardless of gender.

Building a permanent home and life in Colorado over the last few months, I have honed in on fostering my queer community first, which was incredibly terrifying and rewarding. With their compassion and generosity, I have found ethical ways to explore my pansexual identity, and build powerful, loving relationships that challenge my pre-conceived boundaries of what this can mean.

Turns out, who I love can and probably will change over time. More importantly, I can pursue what I need and want, and the world won't fall apart.

Mateo Perez Lara

Diatribe and Rose Thorns

Queer chant:
> Communication is a wish-bone grinded down into
> fractal pieces
> some instance of color is moonlit, so nothing dazzles
> like it should
> I'm wondering if there's good in any of our mouths,
> something decadent
> less proper, wilder & more ridiculous, you took me
> over to this room
> wanted to purify what remained of my queer blood,
> veins stripped
> of their plasma, each golden drip-drop was a way to
> rip me off, rip
> me out, tunnel your way around what didn't make
> you feel swollen
> or erect, like it would've before, I should've stopped
> complaining
> but these eyes were blood-shot and tired and you kept
> talking & taking.

This garden is infested with fire ants, god-awful prayers

that lost my attention the minute they said "burn" what's

absurd is three doors down from my duplex, lives

the world's best figure of Christ, tempted to disinfect my body

of the sins it has committed, must start from the beginning

I'm not one to prioritize which sins were worse, but the best

ones involved cum & youthful glow after men took everything

they stopped believing diamonds originated in this soil

filled with trauma, how do you hold all that lava in your hands

what's burning is that flower I uprooted, what stabbed me

in all its crimson glory, the way the spit sprays from your lips

the mouth washing sin from the air, letting me know

what curse I am in for when I step into hell, I have the key code

I only press enter, now whether I am saintly or sadistic, we have yet

to tell but keep telling me what I am—I'll keep pricking myself on all the flowers.

Mateo Perez Lara

Queer Novena to Lost Things and St. Anthony

without worrying about rent
or being gay or whom to love or straddle or
simply existing without
scarcity of love or trial by fire.

find a tomb where my papa resides
is still alive and fidgeting with anticipation
for the next life—in which he is still protecting

me and my mom and sister and grandma
where he took us to the mountains saved us from
completely drowning in dreams, I'm always the last one

to keep themselves away and awake from terror.

> *"St. Anthony, perfect imitator of Jesus, who*
> *received from God the special power of restoring lost things*
> *grant that I may find Healing from Grief, which has been lost.*

At least restore to me peace and tranquility of mind, the loss of which has afflicted me even more than my material loss. To this favor, I ask another of you: that I may always remain in possession of the true good that is God. Let me rather lose all things than lose God, my supreme good. Let me never suffer the loss of my greatest treasure, eternal life with God. Amen."

each cavity echo like a flashing light pulse hitting steel
a loud chaotic city a dream of my emptiness restored
without any scar or mark still leaving skin raw & bleeding
from pink queer glittery stain on this bare-ribbed chest.

Frank DiPalermo

The Night
Everything Changed

T here was something vaguely Tom of Finland about
my friend Terry. Tom of Finland was a gay artist who
did erotic drawings of handsome men with absurdly muscular
bodies that were often tightly packed into lumberjack shirts.
Terry didn't strongly resemble those men. He was six-two,
mid-forties, slender, had a trim light brown beard, and wore
his thinning hair in a style that was a few years away from being
a comb-over. He did, however, wear a lot of lumberjack shirts,
but they were beside the point. The similarity between Terry
and Tom of Finland was not in their aesthetics, but in their
essence. Neither made any effort to conceal their homosexuality,
their outsized masculinity, or their potent libidos. In fact, they
celebrated those things. Both Terry and Tom of Finland seemed
to think they had nothing to be ashamed of.

This was amazing to me. I was in my mid-twenties when
I met Terry. He was my boyfriend Scott's bestie and they
were both active in gay sports organizations, political groups
and various AIDS charities. I was not. I was so timid about

being gay that I always tried to pass for straight. Which was hilarious, because I actually thought I could pull this off.

Try not to judge me too harshly and I will do likewise. Try to keep in mind that in the early nineties, queer people were targets. One time, my boyfriend and I were walking along Kettner Boulevard in San Diego and I put my hand on his shoulder for maybe three seconds. That's all it took for people in two different cars to yell, "*FAGGOTS!*" That word ripped into me like a bullet and caused all kinds of pain which I pretended not to feel. I was good at pretending because I had a lot of practice. Still, I'd rather avoid pain if given the choice. So, I took my hand off Scott's shoulder. Even now, after twenty years have passed and my boyfriend has become my husband, public displays of affection between us still feel like a dangerous provocation, like waving a piece of raw liver in front of a tiger.

I can't imagine Terry making any concessions in such a situation mainly because I can't picture anyone challenging him in the first place. He was such a potent combination of social gracefulness, genuine friendliness, self-assuredness, bodacious pluck and, well, tallness that he could get away with murder, or at the very least putting his damn hand on his boyfriend's shoulder if he felt like it. Terry, all seventy-four bearded inches of him, once went to a very swanky, very straight fundraising dinner... dressed as Scarlett O'Hara.

This is not to say Terry wasn't careful. When he marched in the Gay Pride Parade, he stayed out of view of the television reporters. Terry had a big, corporate, human resources job. In 1992, it became illegal to fire someone for being gay, so lots of employers took the indirect approach. When they figured out someone was LGBT, they fired them for stealing pencils. Terry really needed his job. Terry really needed his health insurance.

By 1992, I'd had six HIV tests, one each year starting in 1986. Terry had zero. When I asked him about this, he told me in his lilting Tennessee accent, "Why should I get tested? I've had every other damn disease you can get from a dick. Of course, I've got HIV." God, the audacity. Terry just copped to promiscuity, a complicated history with STDs, and made a cavalier assumption about his HIV status, all in a couple of jokey sentences.

I could never do that. Raised in a devout Italian Catholic home, I grew up believing that all sex was shameful, but gay sex was downright demonic. Any diseases associated with it were divine retribution. Growing up gay in a Catholic household taught me how to keep secrets. It did not instill an easy relationship with uneasy truths. I would be more likely to remove my own tonsils with a steak knife than wisecrack about any STDs I might have.

Speaking of uneasy truths: In 1992, there was one proven therapy for AIDS. A drug called AZT extended the life of people with full-blown AIDS by about six months. For people like Terry, people who had the virus but weren't sick yet, there was no protocol, no treatment, no nothing.

Terry couldn't stand doing nothing, so he read every research article he could get his hands on. Then he called the scientists who wrote them: people in Australia, Germany, England, and Atlanta. He was so flipping charming, smart, and persistent, they would often have extended conversations with him. Damned if Terry didn't invent his own anti-AIDS regimen. He took Antabuse, a drug that had helped alcoholics stay sober, because it might have antiviral properties. Vegetable proteins were thought to slow the disease, so he became a vegetarian. He drank a liter of Aloe vera nectar every day. He took vitamins, supplements, herbs, and big fistfuls of pills, at breakfast, lunch, and dinner.

It occurs to me now, with the benefit of hindsight, that Terry's resistance to getting an HIV test and his elaborate alternative health regimen were early evidence of a prowling fear that he kept mostly disguised. It was a disguise that worked on me and perhaps even on Terry himself. His attitude regarding his anti-AIDS routine seemed no different than his attitude toward life in general: optimistic, zestful, and playfully honest.

It's the honesty that has always amazed me. Once, while at dinner with an assortment of friends and acquaintances, Terry plunked his baggie full of pills on the restaurant table and stirred the chalky contents of a different baggie into his water.

"What's all this?" asked Rain, a woman in a breezy peasant dress seated to his left. Terry had met her only a few days before at the organic grocery store. He made friends that easily.

"These," Terry said, picking up the baggie of pills between the first and second finger of his left hand, "are my AIDS zappers." He spilled them onto his palm and downed them with the potion from his water glass. "Well, that's the hope."

Had that been me, I would have invented some sort of spiritual cleanse as an excuse for the pills, the kind of thing you'd hear about from Deepak Choprah. Terry told the absolute truth in a way that rendered Rain momentarily speechless which, I realized as the evening wore on, was not a middling accomplishment.

Terry was playful, but also meticulous. T-cells are the part of the immune system the AIDS virus attacks, and Terry plotted his T-cell counts on a graph. Did their numbers jump after he started drinking the Aloe vera nectar? What about when he added L-lysine to the vitamins he took? Did going vegan have an effect?

Yes, Terry's T-cells did go up a little after he started drinking Aloe vera nectar. Same thing after he started taking

L-lysine, and when he went vegan. These little jumps made me want to celebrate and enabled me to ignore the overall direction of the graph. It never occurred to me, not for a second, that Terry wouldn't beat AIDS. We already had AZT. He just needed to stay healthy until better AIDS drugs came along. And they were coming. Any month, any week, any day, any minute there would be another breakthrough. I could feel it in my bones.

My bones were lying. There wouldn't be any new therapies for AIDS until 1995.

Terry developed something called leukoplakia, a small whitish patch under his tongue which I'm not sure I would have noticed if it were happening to me.

Terry said, "Leukoplakia is a possible precursor to oral cancer." His accent made even the words *oral cancer* slightly musical.

I said, "Terry, you're not going to get cancer."

"Well, I hope you're right. But this is probably my first manifestation of the disease."

I said, "What disease?"

Terry raised an eyebrow, drew his mouth back on one side, and shook his head slowly. "Are you kidding?" he said.

His anti-AIDS regimen got really intense. Every two weeks, he spent a couple of hours inhaling an aerosolized drug that fights the pneumonia associated with AIDS. This made good sense for someone whose immune system was starting to, well, maybe it wasn't working as well as it should. But some of the other things Terry did?

Every Sunday morning, a nurse friend of his threaded a feeding tube up his nose and into his stomach so that cow colostrum could be delivered right to his gut. Colostrum was the stuff mother cows produced just before they started making milk and it boosted the calves' immune systems. Which was great for baby cows, but only the lunatic fringe thought it would have any effect on HIV in humans.

Terry researched Compound Q, an extract from the root of the Chinese cucumber. I remember thinking, *a cucumber is the vegetable equivalent of Wonder Bread. What can it possibly do?* Turns out, a lot. The Chinese used Compound Q to treat cancer and induce late term abortions. It also sometimes caused anaphylactic shock, cardiac arrest, and sudden death. But Terry told me about a study in San Francisco. He said, "It's just in the beginning stages, but Compound Q is powerful medicine. It shows a lot of promise in fighting HIV. I'm going to find out how to get some."

I said, "I don't know, Terry. Those side effects are really scary. Let the study run and see what happens." Terry's eyes opened really wide, and they got really shiny, and I saw the predatory fear stalking inside him. I saw something else too. Terry was thinner.

He never got infused with Compound Q. This was a good thing. Compound Q killed multiple people and was ultimately shown to have no lasting effect against HIV. The reason Terry never did Compound Q was not so good. Terry started puking.

I can't remember if Terry blamed his puking on the vitamins or if I did, but that's what I latched onto: one of the supplements was making him sick. Terry couldn't figure out which one and he had to keep taking them because they were working. He was healthy. Well, except for the leukoplakia and the weight loss. And then he had another whitish area in his mouth that was probably thrush. Aside from those things, Terry was healthy. He could live with the barfing every once in a while. We could all live with Terry barfing once in a while. Except pretty soon, it was a couple of times a week. Then every day.

Then the headaches started. Terrible headaches. When they hit, his face turned gray. Thank God, they usually didn't last long. Until the one that did.

One Saturday afternoon, my boyfriend Scott and I got a call from a friend who was a massage therapist. He said, "There's a message from Terry on my answering machine. He's got a headache and he thinks a massage will cure it. He sounds really bad. Like really sick."

Scott and I called Terry and got no answer. We stopped by his house, but no one was there. Other people contacted us. Karen got a voicemail from Terry and "he sounded awful." So did Jim. So did Bob. Everyone was worried, but no one spoke directly to him, and no one knew where he was. I worried too, but I was not out of my mind. I mean, this was Terry. He probably checked himself into a hospital and we just didn't know which one.

Wrong. As sick as he was, Terry had arranged to have dinner with a friend. And as sick as he was, he drove to that friend's apartment. By the time he got there, his headache was so bad, he had no choice but to lie down. Then it got even worse, and he couldn't stand back up. Scott and I found him lying on a couch with the lights off, the shades drawn, and every curtain pulled tight. He had a cold compress on his eyes and his skin was the color of a dirty dishrag. It looked like he was going to die right in front of us if he didn't get to a hospital. My heart pounded, my breath went shallow, gooseflesh broke out on my forearms. In other words, I was panicking.

Terry was not. He lifted a corner of the compress and looked at Scott and me. "Well, look what the Burmese Python dragged in. We were going to dinner, only I got a headache and I'm waiting for it to pass."

Scott said, "Hey, Terry."

Terry said, "I'd like to go to that vegetarian restaurant on El Cajon Boulevard, but I'm hesitant because the last time their tortilla chips tasted like bug spray."

He went on and on about how the new owners of Cornucopia wrecked the only good vegetarian restaurant in San Diego. He was profoundly sick, yet mustered enough energy not just to talk, but to banter. I began to realize there was something much more powerful at work than his suffering. The panther-ish fear I'd gotten glimpses of earlier, now owned him and ruled him.

He did not want to go to the hospital and wouldn't allow the conversation to swerve near the topic. I imagine it felt like a capitulation to him, an acknowledgement that despite his vegetarianism, his vitamins, his Aloe vera nectar, his cow colostrum, his pneumocystis pneumonia treatments, and his relentless good humor, he could not defeat HIV. He probably worried that if he went to the hospital, he would not come home. I would have.

Scott kept trying, but Terry was tenacious and wouldn't let him get a word in edgewise. A different tactic was required. Perhaps a broadside of plainspoken truth from an unexpected source would pierce his defenses. There was only one problem. The unexpected source would have to be me. I was not strong and far from easy with uneasy truths. That described Terry. But he was sick and weak and scared. He needed someone to be like he was before he got sick. I wasn't sure if I could rise to the occasion, but there were no other options. I took a deep breath and blurted out, "Terry, you need to go to the hospital. Right now. We're going to take you."

Doesn't seem like much, does it? But that one sentence laid it bare. Terry was different. He needed to be taken care of because for the first time since I'd known him, he couldn't take care of himself. He fought us a little bit, but not much. He was too weak for that. And he might have been relieved.

We got him to the ER, and I took his insurance card to the front desk to check him in. Next to me was a handsome young man who was so sick with AIDS that he could barely breathe. He was all by himself, checking into a hospital. He must have been so scared. He must have felt so alone. I tried to smile at him, but an orderly came with a wheelchair and took him away.

In the early nineties, none of this was unusual. For an emergency room in a city with a good-sized gay population, this was just another Tuesday evening.

Terry did not die that night. Turned out he had an AIDS-related lesion on his brain, and it was swelling. They started him on steroids and anti-inflammatory drugs. He felt better within hours and went home a few days later.

He had some good days after all this. Not many, but some. About four weeks later, he died at home, surrounded by family and friends.

So.

It's not the early nineties anymore. We have elected officials, movie stars, business leaders, and Olympic athletes who are out and proud members of the LGBTQ community. I legally married my wonderful boyfriend, Scott. AIDS has become a manageable condition. But I don't want to forget what it was like not that long ago. I want to remember the handsome young man who stood next to me when I checked Terry into the hospital, because I'm not sure anyone else does. I want to remember Terry, the person who was living the truth while I was living secrets. I want to remember these men, and I want you to remember them, too.

Joan McNamara

Sexy High Heels

It was early October 2010 and I was fifty-nine years old.
I was in Monterey in a trendy consignment shop with my
seventeen-year-old niece, Erika. Her mom had asked me to
take her shopping for some new school clothes. As Auntie
Joan, I couldn't refuse.

Erika was a senior in High School. That August, Erika had
started hormone therapy for her transition to a woman. Fall
break was coming up, and Erika wanted to return to school
wearing feminine clothes for the first time.

Erika's parents had concerns for her safety, especially outside of school. They were worried Erika might be discriminated
against or treated unkindly. Their worst fear was that Erika might
even be attacked. Her parents understood their fears would probably ruin Erika's shopping spree, so they recruited me.

Erika found a number of skirts to try on and took them into
the dressing room. I was wandering around the shop when my
eyes fell upon a pair of sexy grey snakeskin high heels. I was
immediately transported back to November 1985.

I was thirty-five years old on an airplane wearing my favorite sexy red snakeskin high heels. After the plane took off, I

glanced across the aisle. There sat a very handsome guy, about my age, reading Charles Dickens' *Great Expectations*. He looked up, noticed me, and said, "I like those shoes."

We talked all the way to San Diego and have been together ever since.

I wondered if I should buy the heels for Erika. What would her dad, a retired Navy Commander, actually think? He had never seen Erika in feminine clothes, let alone a pair of sexy high heels.

Erika came out of the dressing room modelling a skirt she liked. She twirled around and had a wonderful smile on her face. I showed her the shoes and her eyes lit up. She knew the story about my snakeskin heels. She tried them on and tentatively walked around the shop. She was quite unsteady, but beaming the whole time.

We left the store with the skirt and shoes and went to lunch. I felt so proud that Erika's parents trusted me to take her on this shopping spree. My heart was full of pride for Erika. She was bravely transitioning to the woman she was meant to be.

The next day I asked Erika how her mom and dad liked her new clothes. Especially, I wondered how her dad felt about the high heels. Well, he told her. "I think the skirt is too short, but I like those shoes."

Never, ever underestimate the power of a pair of sexy high heels!

Bradley Dyer

Tony

I **still remember when I met Tony, and I always will.** The image is burned into my mind as both a fond recollection and a moment of utter regret.

I had chatted with him for several days on Grindr and I was so intrigued. The feeling was mutual, and we agreed that he would come to the gas station where I worked to meet. He had sent me pictures of himself, but I was so utterly unprepared for the beautiful man that walked through the door that sunny afternoon in Detroit. His hair was dark, his skin olive, and his eyes contained a spark that was somehow both calming and exhilarating. He wore blue jeans and a white t-shirt, just like the Lana Del Rey song, and when he smiled at me, I melted inside and felt weak in the knees.

We talked outside for a bit by the tow trucks on my lunch break. And that night, he picked me up from work. I thought he was the most charming guy that I had ever met. We spent that night together, and in the morning when he drove me home, he held my hand.

At the time, I was not fully out of the closet. I had never felt comfortable with my sexuality. But Tony told me I was beautiful. He made me feel special in a life that I had walked through feeling invisible. I felt noticed, I felt visible, and I finally felt like somebody recognized my particularity.

We would talk for hours. It was the most any man had ever wanted to know about me. Every word I spoke seemed to captivate him. When we fucked, I swear to God, I had never felt so alive. He awakened something inside of me. For what seemed like the first time, I felt fucking passion. For once in my life, I felt free. I had buried so much of who I was so deep inside that I often didn't recognize myself. But when he touched me, when I touched him, I saw that person again. I felt like I had reunited with some long-lost part of myself. For me, that was a freedom I had waited a long time to find.

I had never been in love, but whatever I felt for Tony was the closest I had ever come.

Seemingly overnight, things changed. It became evident that Tony knew how much I liked him. Once he knew he had me, I became something he took for granted. Shamelessly, I crawled back every time. When he criticized my clothes, I listened, and bought new ones. When he criticized my appearance, I cut my hair, I worked out, I moisturized, I shaved. When he made me feel ashamed to be myself, when he embarrassed me in front of his friends, when he criticized my friends, I laid down and I let him.

I awoke late one night after we had gone out and I overheard him talking to his roommate Ron. I knew instantly that he was talking about me. I could hear him saying that he didn't like the way that I dressed, that I didn't have a car, and that he always wound up falling in love with losers. He told Ron that he didn't think I had any drive and that he didn't think I had much of a future. I don't know if he thought I was sleeping, out of earshot, or if he simply had no regard for my feelings.

But once again, desperate to be wanted, desperate to be loved, I lied in bed and told myself I'd heard wrong.

Another night, while I was grabbing drinks for us at a bar, I noticed he was caught up in a heated conversation with a young guy, a guy very similar-looking to me. I could hear him trying to appeal to Tony. I could hear the desperation in his voice as he pleaded for Tony to please come outside and talk to him. I could see the pain, the fear, the familiar yearning in his eyes as he said, almost crying, "Tony, this isn't you. You're a nice guy. How could you do this?" Then I heard it, that moment I should have seen as my cue to leave, the red flag to end this one sided love affair. I heard Tony utter so clearly one sentence over the thud of the bass. "Because I'm not a good person."

When I approached, he threw his arm around me and kissed me. It felt so good, so good that my mind stopped spiralling and all I could think was, "He wants me." I could see hurt in this other guy's eyes, I could see his desperation, and sadly enough, I could completely empathize. Tony was breaking someone's heart, using me as a prop to do it, but still I could not or would not look at what was happening right in front of me. That night, I got incredibly drunk to cope with a feeling that I could not shake and hadn't the capacity to articulate.

I felt so hurt. Still, I ditched my friends to leave with him. We got to his apartment and I let him fuck me. But for the first night since our short acquaintance began, he didn't grab me and pull me close to him. He didn't kiss me, he didn't press his body against mine. Afterwards, he didn't grab my hand or wrap his legs around mine. He simply turned over, told me he had to be up at 6:00 a.m. to go to the gym, and he fell asleep.

As I laid next to Tony, I thought about the value I had placed on him, how much power I had given this individual. I had allowed this guy to dictate how I felt about myself. I had allowed him to use me, mistreat me, and disrespect me. Still, I felt like I loved him. But in my heart, I knew the truth: Tony would never ever love me. Not for a second.

I wish I could say that I sat up, pulled on my jeans, collected the shattered remnants of my dignity, and left. But I didn't. I turned over to face the other direction, and silently I cried. I knew in that moment that I needed to leave, I knew that he didn't want me like I wanted him. It wasn't until Tony ghosted me that I began to understand how to separate the fantasy of what our short acquaintance meant to me, from the reality of what it meant to him.

I used to think that all that Tony ever gave to me was six months of low self-esteem and an irrational STD phobia. He definitely used me, that much is true. But the fact is, I used him too. I used his body to make myself feel sexy. I used his charm, his confidence, his security, to facilitate my own coming out during our "relationship." He broke my fragile and fickle heart, but for that I now thank him. Because he showed me it was possible to love, that I was able to feel attractive and seen. He awoke passion in me for the first time in my life. After the sadness of rejection had passed, hope emerged. The hope that one day I would find someone, and we'd make each other feel special, noticed, and beautiful.

He also taught me a more valuable lesson, perhaps the most valuable lesson of all. I learned that until I gained some semblance of self-possession, until I learned the power of self-validation, I would never ever be healthy enough to find peace within any relationship. I needed to find room on that pedestal I had built for him—room for myself.

Raine Grayson

We Are All Becoming A Gamble— Remembering Pulse & the Queer History of Mourning

I try to write about the June 12th, 2016 Pulse Orlando nightclub shooting every year, but it never feels right. The tributes, plays, and poems never feel as though they can properly honor the forty-nine killed and fifty-three wounded. So I *backspace, backspace, backspace* until I eventually find myself silent once again.

This year, however, I stumbled upon the journal entries I wrote on the days surrounding Pulse—scrawled after pages of inconsequential to-do lists, appointment reminders, and doodles, concretizing how incomprehensible a massacre of such magnitude was up until that day. I was twenty-four at the time, constantly hopping between my home in upstate

New York and my long-distance partner's place in New Jersey. In 2016, I was at the apex of my queerness. I had just come out as a trans man and started hormone therapy, was freshly in love, and made my side cash as a drag king. It was, I thought, a great time to be queer.

June 12th, 2016
The day of the Orlando shooting.
I don't know what to say. I have no clue how to write or respond to what has happened in my lifetime.
I know it could be any of us. I know that at any time any of us could be lost.
I vow to give up on petty infighting and love the people in my life—from all walks.
We have all done wrong, but we must hold tight to each other and fight another day.
There's something incredible about public spaces that are split down the middle. I'm in a diner in NJ. Right now Fox News is playing Trump talking to Bill O'Reilly. Someone who is eating in here supports Trump. I can tell by the sticker on their car outside. I feel unsafe—and because of that, I'm forced to hold my head high and look forward. In my diners at home I can do whatever the glittery hell I want. But you never know. You can never know if a bar will be safe or not. You can never tell if a diner, a store, someone's parents will be safe. Public life is a necessary gamble.
Social media has become part of this public web of unsafety-safety.
We are all becoming a gamble.

The day of the shooting, I was at work. Bustling hard around my little cafe, I had no connection to the outside world, and my mostly conservative clientele gave me no clue during my seven-hour shift. It was the day of the Tony Awards—I was dreaming about what snacks I would make for the viewing party for me and my friends. The minute I got out of work, it all flooded in.

As always, I spent a few minutes in my car drying off the sweat after a long day before heading home. Idly, I checked my phone.

Hey y'all. Are you going to the vigil tonight?
Panicked, I respond:
I literally just got off work. I have no clue what's going on. Vigil for what?

The responses are burned into me forever.
For the shooting that happened in Orlando early this morning. If you go on FB you'll see it.
50+ killed. At a gay bar.

I did check Facebook and was met with a wall of eulogies. I scrolled and scrolled as I felt my body become more and more numb with disbelief. I couldn't cry. I couldn't move. All I could do was sit in my car and stare out the window and think: "But it's such a beautiful day." It is the feeling you get when your life is irreversibly changed and as you watch the world around you, it makes no sense to you that the earth continues to turn and the sun continues to shine. In your heart of hearts, you know that the skies should open up into pouring rain and rolling clouds. It feels inappropriate for the sun to shine.

Eventually, I drove home. I don't remember starting the car, turning into my driveway, or opening my front door, but it must have happened. My roommate at the time was home when I got there. She was also queer and I didn't have to ask if she heard the news or not—I could see on her face that she had been living in this new cruel world for hours.

Our apartment lived in silence as we tried to continue our day. She cooked dinner in disbelief. I showered in disbelief. We sat on the couch and stared at the wall in disbelief.

I originally flip-flopped between going to the vigil being held in a small local park—I was afraid to be surrounded by so much sadness—but I eventually cancelled on my Tony viewing and headed down. My then long-distance partner, now the fiancé who I live with, drove nearly three hours to attend with me. We couldn't bear being apart. We don't know how to articulate the fear we feel as we grasp each other as tightly as we can the minute their car pulls into my lot. We squeeze and squeeze and squeeze. It could have been either of us. We don't have to say it out loud, but we know. And as selfish and as heartless as it sounds, I thank whatever God that will listen that they are alive.

I don't remember exactly how many people attended, but there were over 100 that came and went, and at least fifty or sixty people who remained throughout. People had created a heart out of tea lights around a small printed paper that read a memorandum for the victims. Flowers were laid around the site and people stood huddled together in the wind, holding their candles and their loved ones close. I knew almost everyone.

I remember at one point looking up and counting forty-nine heads at random; that was the amount of friends I would have lost. The number felt impossible.

The night was silent except for crying and howling wind. The air was too heavy, and when people tried to smile or crack a joke to help cut the darkness, no one could bring themselves to find the joy. I hugged people I hadn't spoken to in years. I hugged everybody that showed up. Every once in a while, someone would burst out in tears, and the masses would swoop in to comfort them. I was greeting someone who had just arrived, and saw out of the corner of my eye my partner crumple, then disappear in a mass of support. We were literally holding each other up.

In times of crisis, I try to put myself on the frontline and do everything I can to help. Earlier on in the same week I was standing outside of a local business with a handful of other LGBTQIA+ people and allies, a business that had discriminated against a trans friend, shouting them down and passing out water. So I came to the vigil ready to be a pillar of support however I could... but the reality of it was this wasn't a protest. It was a vigil. There was nothing to do except stand together as a community and keep the candles lit.

WHEN I LOOK BACK ON the night of the vigil, I feel connections between that moment and the queer history of mourning.

I picture Marsha P. Johnson's vigil.

I've spent night after night learning everything I can about Marsha P. Johnson—a founder of the Gay Liberation Front, a trans woman of color, and one of the first of many at the Stonewall Inn during the 1969 riots that changed the course of queer history forever. I've pored over books written about her and watched archival footage until I am drawn to tears in admiration. She is my hero.

She was found dead in the Hudson River in 1992.

When I watch footage of her vigil for a project many years later, I realize that *I can feel myself there*. Post-Pulse, it doesn't feel like I'm looking back on history anymore, but instead like I've become a part of it.

I can smell the musty river water—a smell that hangs over the same town our Pulse vigil was held in. There is something about mourning that is so evocative and timeless, it feels as though by holding my candle for Pulse, *I held my candle for Marsha.*

I look down at the impromptu memorial created for her. I take my turn in helping to form it, placing an empty liquor bottle next to a handmade poster which outlines the shape of her body where it has been dragged out of the river. I watch as others instantly fill the bottle with branches of evergreen. The poster of Marsha, looking so shoddy and saintlike, feels nightmarishly similar to the ones handed out for Pulse victims.

Randy Wicker is videotaping us all. Street youth are eulogizing, telling long-winded personal stories about all of the ways Marsha had changed them. As the community comes together to remember Marsha with stories—in a way we were unable to at our vigil—it's hard not to be angry, guilty, and grief stricken. The victims of Pulse did not and will not receive such personalized community eulogies. With so many people gone at once, there are simply not enough hours in a night.

BUT THEN I PICTURE THE immensity of the AIDS Memorial Quilt—the 48,000+ panel quilt to display and memorialize more than 100,000 AIDS victims, begun in 1985. My community tried to make beauty in memoriam and also tried to make change, with tears in our eyes and loss in our hearts. Each panel was crafted lovingly by a loved one left behind, and together each individual memory has created a 1.3 million square foot reminder that each victim was loved. Perhaps I should feel comforted. The quilt is a reminder that no matter how many of us are lost, we will remember. We will become unforgettable.

It's not fair. I've done so much research and have committed so much of my time to ensuring the safety of myself and my community, and it took only one man—*one man*—to remind me that I am fragile in this world. The very act of existing as gay and trans means I am a target. It doesn't matter how many times I read about my community's activism and take actions to protect our rights and ability to live; one man can take out forty-nine of our voices in one night.

I think about how many shootings have happened since the Pulse vigil. I think about the seemingly endless violence enacted upon trans people.

A trans woman neighbor of mine received threatening letters left on her house for more than a year. They almost comically resembled a cartoonish representation of what a death threat should be: words clipped out of magazines to spell out the word "faggot." The letters called her an abomination, said that she belonged in Hell. She stood strong, proudly raising her pride flags on her porch and refusing to back down. One day, she found her beloved cat severed in half in the woods outside her house. The police helped prove that it was a man-made cut. The town we shared was supposedly very liberal. This happened down the street from the little bar that turned into a pop-up queer meetup once a week. We thought we had found sanctuary.

Forty-nine voices. One night. We are lucky to survive.

I MOVED FROM SAID LIBERAL town to a conservative suburb in New Jersey. Ironically, I made the move to live with my fiancé, who is also trans. I want to revel in planning our marriage and our future together, but instead I am afraid to apply for a job because there is a confederate flag hanging on a house down the street and someone in the neighborhood mows his lawn with a handgun in his holster. I can't help but think of my old neighbor. I can't help but think about the threats and assaults that were hurled at *me* as I became more visible and open about, and in, my trans body. I think about how badly I do not want to get shot and how badly I do not want the ones I love to get shot. The news stations and Twitter tell me it is only a matter of time, and until then I am just one of the lucky ones. I think about how I do not want to be in public because being in public at all means *I am open for attack*. My old therapist told me I was making it all up in my head when I told her about the time an old couple stared at me like I was a zoo animal and I feared for my life. I didn't know how to tell her it is because of couples like that that I have to come to terms with being afraid every time I am celebrating or proud.

I can't stop being proud, though. I feel the constant need to celebrate, even in the wake of so much fear and destruction. I am so in love with my queer life. I look into my partner's eyes and I see what the future can look like. I think about the children we will raise and how those children will spend every moment of their life affirmed and open. I look at myself in the mirror and marvel at the way hormone replacement therapy has changed my body into something I adore. It was only a few weeks before the Pulse shooting that I was dancing in the clubs with all of my friends, unapologetically covered in glitter and sweat and glowing with happiness. Is it ironic that when I exist in these spaces I feel untouchable? I know there is a queer future, because every step I take brings me closer to it. Even if I'm always aware of the fact that one man could end it, my thoughts don't stop the future from being bold and bright and *there*. I feel like I owe it to everyone who isn't as lucky as I am to live the *hell* out of my queer future. As I look at my journals, I think about how to be queer is to be in a constant state of mourning and to never get too comfortable, because soon there will be another wave of death. To be queer is to constantly be on the outskirts or in the middle of an epidemic of death. To be queer is to know death personally.

But then I turn the journal's page, and there is a love letter to my fiancé. And I also remember that to be queer is to live knowing the meaning of divine happiness. To be queer is to develop the superhuman trait of knowing exactly who you are meant to be. To be queer is to never be forgotten. We share a strength eternal.

To THE VICTIMS OF THE Pulse Orlando shooting:
I will never forget you.
We will never forget you.
Rest in peace, and rest in power.
Your spirits will always be with me.

Stanley Almodovar III, 23 years old
Amanda L. Alvear, 25 years old
Oscar A. Aracena-Montero, 26 years old
Rodolfo Ayala-Ayala, 33 years old
Antonio Davon Brown, 29 years old
Darryl Roman Burt II, 29 years old
Angel L. Candelario-Padro, 28 years old
Juan Chevez-Martinez, 25 years old
Luis Daniel Conde, 39 years old
Cory James Connell, 21 years old
Tevin Eugene Crosby, 25 years old
Deonka Deidra Drayton, 32 years old

Simón Adrian Carrillo Fernández, 31 years old
Leroy Valentin Fernandez, 25 years old
Mercedez Marisol Flores, 26 years old
Peter Ommy Gonzalez-Cruz, 22 years old
Juan Ramon Guerrero, 22 years old
Paul Terrell Henry, 41 years old
Frank Hernandez, 27 years old
Miguel Angel Honorato, 30 years old
Javier Jorge-Reyes, 40 years old
Jason Benjamin Josaphat, 19 years old
Eddie Jamoldroy Justice, 30 years old
Anthony Luis Laureano Disla, 25 years old
Christopher Andrew Leinonen, 32 years old
Alejandro Barrios Martinez, 21 years old
Brenda L. Marquez McCool, 49 years old
Gilberto R. Silva Menendez, 25 years old
Kimberly Jean Morris, 37 years old
Akyra Monet Murray, 18 years old
Luis Omar Ocasio-Capo, 20 years old
Geraldo A. Ortiz-Jimenez, 25 years old
Eric Ivan Ortiz-Rivera, 36 years old
Joel Rayon Paniagua, 32 years old
Jean Carlos Mendez Perez, 35 years old
Enrique L. Rios, Jr., 25 years old
Jean Carlos Nieves Rodríguez, 27 years old
Xavier Emmanuel Serrano Rosado, 35 years old
Christopher Joseph Sanfeliz, 24 years old
Yilmary Rodríguez Solivan, 24 years old
Edward Sotomayor Jr., 34 years old
Shane Evan Tomlinson, 33 years old
Martin Benitez Torres, 33 years old
Jonathan A. Camuy Vega, 24 years old

Juan Pablo Rivera Velázquez, 37 years old
Luis Sergio Vielma, 22 years old
Franky Jimmy DeJesus Velázquez, 50 years old
Luis Daniel Wilson-Leon, 37 years old
Jerald Arthur Wright, 31 years old

Y.L. Schmeltz

Hidden Presence

My other name is
    a long list
    hidden
in the sand, where glass is made under all this pressure.

But really, probably, i need a spell.
A spell that lands my open, unbroken heart back in my body
except
it's not unbroken.
I'm better for it
    is what i tell myself.
The moment it shattered in so many pieces
wrapped up and warped around love and death for over a decade.
Maybe that sand pressure, that sand pressure where my other
names are,
maybe that is what my heart needs.
    bleeds before people
    making honest messes
    for piling, crawling, mounting, feeling
the weight of love lost on organ after organ after organ
pressed upon the in-betweens of my skin folds
just to keep other cold hands warm.

Where's the spell?
How do i work with my still waves?
Stuck in the earth, mud wrapped ankles uncovered
leaving just that dry layer of crusty dirt, stiffened hairs, to
honor the journey.
Bending knees,
asking for undeserved forgiveness
~~heart of a home or~~
~~the home of a heart...~~
either way, it was real.

My heart is my only real home, hollow for the making.
i carry in my chest
        a deep, cavern of warmth
          where hearts hibernate before giving birth
              to heavy blooded butch rain.
bind
bound
spun
sung in the sweet green wind of when
        when i was home
        when i was held

When
        interrupted by living pillars of life
staring down the paths that seemingly lead to all the same place.

Just in case we forget the massive blue sky and its
interwoven immensity
to remind that all things small can also be big
and the reminder grows in yellow blankets of soft petals
covering a whole row of life lived

with increments of
        intensity,
                unforgettable desire,
                        not built to be put in rows
Something is not linear,
and yet here I am in the middle of life,
of the here and
now.
Plucked, prodded, and poked by birth and death to be reminded
of my positionality.

The sound of wooo hoos, and cooos, and bells dinging faintly,
next to a persistent and insistent chugging train whistle, voices
solemnly sweep through the breeze.
Small things, thread together, creating something to feel small again.
To see all of our working pieces together in the
        sunned same place.

Back to presence, no more "shoulds."
Only…
        wish, want, could.
Perhaps that's why presence is indelible
mark making
        on bodies breathing to be felt and heard, not named
                or claimed
renamed over and over and over again
reclaiming shame in the same way that it's slathered about

Here in the middle is presence,
        what comes before, predicates what comes next,
                letters, sounds, the way your tongue moves
                across the page

a muscle
it comes in stages
if you could lick my brain, would that be sexy?
I'd settle for someone sweetly kissing my thoughts.

JD Burke

The Bad Gay

When I was young, I was an asshole.

At the age of seventeen, I moved in with my Grandparents so I could go to college. Grandma was a Norwegian ice princess: beautiful, stoic, and silently terrifying. Grandpa was a funny, loudmouthed Italian with a curly mustache and a kind of regressive charm—a sort of Guido caveman. We drove from my childhood home in Colorado to San Diego in his old '66 Chevy pickup. We stayed in shitty motels, read the *Weekly World News*, told dirty jokes, and drank Snapple while the miles rumbled past. Snapple was still a thing then.

When we crossed the California state border and the "Welcome to California" sign appeared, Granddad suddenly became serious.

"Son, there are three rules you need to abide to stay under our roof," he said, never taking his eyes off the road.

"Keep your grades up," he admonished gravely. I nodded.

"Always respect your Grandma," he warned. "Women should always be respected."

I nodded.

"No fat girls in the pool," he said, and snickered. I rolled my eyes.

In high school I started to have dreams about guys. I began to notice certain feelings. But I couldn't allow myself to indulge them. They scared the shit out of me. I didn't know how to be a man that had these feelings.

Instead I wrenched on old cars with Grandpa, started lifting weights, listened to heavy metal, skated, rode a motorcycle, dated girls. I did dude things. But women confused me. Relationships would end abruptly because I said the wrong thing—or hadn't said anything. Nothing seemed straightforward or easy, and my love life was a constant. Mess. Something inside me was changing. I was losing integrity between the man I wanted to be, the man everyone expected me to be, and the man I was becoming.

But I kept trying.

In college I got a job at a mom and pop business. I'd been there for a year or so when, out of the blue, the wife… came onto me. I came home from work that night, quietly bewildered. Another encounter with the ladies gone inexplicably wrong. I leaned heavily against the kitchen counter in the semi darkness, alone with my confusion. I had been raised by quintessential men. But they could not help me now. Dad was three states away. Grandpa was here, but he was—well, he was Grandpa. And he was asleep.

But not for long. He tottered out of his bedroom in his customary saggy tighty whities to get a glass of water. When he saw me brooding in the shadows, he asked me what was wrong. I told him about the night I had just had. He listened patiently. I felt grateful to share his company just then, to talk together as men. Then he put his hand on my shoulder and said, "I'm sorry, son."

"Thanks Grandpa," I said, and he patted my shoulder consolingly before making another, less comforting proclamation.

"I'm disappointed in you."

If I'd had anything in my mouth besides bitter exhaustion, I would have spit it across the room. "What?" I asked, shocked. "Why the hell are you disappointed in me???"

"You didn't bang her!" he said, eyes wide, arms outspread in disbelief.

"Grandpa! She's my boss! She's twice my age!"

"Son, you're a young man, and these broads need service!" His fist stabbed the air with Italian emphasis. "You have to service these horny broads! I would have!"

"Grandpa, she's MARRIED," I protested indignantly. "She has a husband and a KID." But he had already turned back to the bedroom, muttering and shaking his head. He gave me one final piece of Grandpa George wisdom.

"Goddammit, son. A ring doesn't close a hole."

A ring. Doesn't close. A hole. From the mouths of seventy-year-olds.

I realized what had to happen next. No. More. Broads. It was time to jump into the deep end of homo lake. I was bad at girls. I couldn't possibly be worse at guys.

I came out of the closet at age 23, and I was a terrible gay. I came from a family of incorrigible badasses. My dad was the epitome of red-blooded heterosexuality: a Vietnam Veteran, a one-time Sergeant at Arms in the Mongols, a carpenter, a bruiser, and a shitkicker. I was his oldest son. I wasn't gay. I couldn't be. I hated bars and clubs. Drag queens were terrifying to me, like vicious, gender-fuck sharknadoes. I couldn't put an outfit together or dance worth a shit. But I was gay. And I was bad at it.

My first real boyfriend looked like a storybook prince. He was tall, blond, and handsome, and he spoke with a southern accent that charmed everyone he met. *I...* did not look like a storybook prince. I looked more like a villain. "All hail Damien!" my friends would say when I walked into a room. I was a brooder. I had rough edges. I used them to shield myself against this new, terrifying part of my identity and to deflect others that exemplified it. I wasn't gay, I just happened to like guys. I was different. I didn't fit in. I was a dude apart. A singular man. A lone wolf. With no equal.

I was a homophobic tool. And I was a lot worse at guys. I had a big ego and low self esteem, which, it turns out, is a super awesome combo for attracting quality men. Brian, my storybook prince, turned out to be more of a frog. We hadn't been together more than a few months when the three ways started. I was in love with him and I only wanted him. He wanted to sleep with other men. One day he gave me an ultimatum.

"I'll either do it with you, or do it without you."

I loved him. I wanted to make it work. I tried things his way. For a while.

When the day finally came, I moved out so suddenly, I had to live in my shitty hatchback until I found a new place. Brian offered me a room. My pride would not allow me to stay. I put my belongings in storage and rolled around San Diego for a while, living in my ride. Like Jewel before she got a record deal. But with drier lips.

The next romantic abortion was Dev. He was not a bastard. He was funny and cute and he doted on me. He looked like a pint-sized Tom Cruise—and ultimately he turned out to be just as crazy. But we had so much in common. My family lived in Tucson. Dev's family lived in Tucson. I was a personal trainer. He went to the gym. He was a Buddhist. I liked the Beastie Boys. It was going to work between us, I just knew it.

Oh, the fights. The glorious fights. I read a newspaper during a flight to Lake Tahoe, which to Dev meant I was "shutting him out." He gave me the silent treatment for the first 24 hours of the trip, and then told me he was taking me to the airport so he could enjoy what was left of our weekend—alone. I responded with icy Scandinavian calm and began packing my things. But this just stoked his anger. "You're not going ANYWHERE!" he screamed, and grabbed me roughly by the arms. In a blind rage I picked him up and tossed him on the bed. It squeaked once under his weight, almost comically, and then he cried for two hours while I walked in the blinding snow, waiting for my fury to cool.

Of course, we married soon after that.

Kidding.

I could not understand what the problem was. I was a catch, wasn't I? I was a personal trainer and an EMT. I was educated and funny and a great cook. I had all the cool "masc dude bro" things you'd put in your online dating profile. I could fix things. I could build things. Just not a relationship worth a shit.

I swore off love for a while. It wasn't. Working. Mommy issues: check. Daddy issues: check. Gay son with a handful of failed relationships and an unshakeable feeling that there was nobody out there for him: checkmate.

Grad school would be my new lover. I threw myself into my studies. I couldn't make love work, but my education, my career—what could go wrong?

I got laid off at my job. I was fucked.

Obviously, once I graduated with a Master of Fine Arts in Film, I'd be knee-deep in money, fame, and Hollywood job offers. But at that moment, I felt wretched and hopeless.

Wayne, a coworker, came to my rescue. He was an older gay man, quiet, polite, and kind-hearted. I had no money. He rented me a room for three hundred and fifty dollars. I went to college. He lived in the college area. I was lazy. He had a pool. Score.

On a Saturday morning, shortly after I moved in, I rolled out of bed in my underwear and stumbled sleepily towards the bathroom. A woman who looked like old-timey Elizabeth Taylor was standing in front of the mirror, primping her hair. I apologized to her for my near nakedness.

"Sorry Ma'am. I didn't realize Wayne had guests." She looked at me. She was beautiful. She was glamorous. She… was a man.

"JD, it's Wayne," she intoned in a voice too deep to be made by lady parts. A chill ran down my spine. I was living with a drag queen.

Life went on. I got over my fear of drag queens because I lived with one. Turns out, those bitches are hilarious. In film school I was surrounded by flamboyant creative types—actors and the like—and I got over my fear of them, too. I made friends. I tried wearing pink once.

I stopped taking myself so seriously and loosened up. A little.

I also got lonely. I wanted to meet someone. But I was terribly suited to meeting people. I hated bars and other settings where such meetings would be probable. For all my progress, I still battled with the misanthropic jerk inside who didn't get along with other gay men. I looked for all the things we didn't have in common. I found reasons we were different. I judged. I created distance. I was a terrible gay. I was a gay Betta Fish.

There were a few short-lived flings but nothing stuck. I broke it off every time. Nobody seemed quite right. I persisted in my studies, all the while hoping, with quiet yearning, that I'd meet the right guy.

But the degree program dragged on. After a couple of thesis extensions, I realized I was using my education as a reason not to become involved with someone. It was convenient bullshit. "I like you, I do, I just have to focus on my education right now." It was a familiar refrain. I had once broken up with a guy because, as I told him, "I think you're a great guy, I really do. But I really need to focus on my Martial Arts training right now." I was That Asshole. I was That Guy who said Those Things. I... was a douchefag.

The irony struck me hard. *I* wasn't the right guy. I had complained loudly about unavailable twats, not realizing until years had passed that I was one of them. I was the King of Unavailable Twats.

This revelation was a tectonic shift in my life. I don't push gay people away any more. I treasure my gay friends, which are many now. I think drag queens are hilarious and fascinating. I love divey gay bars for the cheap drinks and the great people watching.

And when I just fucking RELAXED and stopped trying to meet Mr. Right, I actually met him. His name is Vinse. With an S. That's sexy, right?

Vinse is my best friend. We spoil each other. We have fun. We annoy each other on purpose and play what my Dad calls "grabass!" We have the same sick sense of humor, and I love his dogs, and he cuddles like a champ. We watch *Rupaul's Drag Race*—and then we watch *Vikings*. He takes me out to bars to go dancing, and I take him out to the desert to go camping. We call each other "baybay" and "tiger" and "punkin" and other things so cute and disgusting my friends threaten to puke when they hear it.

And I don't fucking care.

Grandpa likes him. Grandma... would have liked him too. I love him.

I was wrong. Being with guys hasn't been easier. But it's better. And I still don't really fit in. But that's not because I'm gay.

Some people would say I'm still an asshole. But fuck those people. Love isn't always sweet, but it sustains me. I love, and I am loved. Exactly the way I am.

Contributors

Henry Aronson is a second generation Filipino American. This is his first attempt at creative writing. He is a professor at a local college where he teaches English. He's a native Californian and is happily married to his husband.

Kelly Bowen (she/her/hers) is a longtime bass guitarist and Berklee alumna turned writer. Multiple performances in So Say We All's VAMP shows as well as at Poets Underground hooked her on the written word, as well as led to her first poetry publications: in Poets Underground's *Fuck Isolation: A Tribute to the Covid-19 Experience* and in the forthcoming *2020-21 San Diego Poetry Annual.* Clearly suffering from workaholism, in addition to her music activities, she continues to write memoirs and poetry, has recently branched into speculative fiction, and is currently editing her first novel. For more info, please see: Kellybowenarts.com.

Mickey Brent grew up in California, but has lived most of her adult life in Europe. Her first lesbian romance novel, *Underwater Vibes*, and its sequel, *Broad Awakening*, take place in Brussels, Belgium. Mickey has published numerous travel adventures, short stories, and articles under various pseudonyms. She is currently tweaking her third novel, set in San Francisco, starring a diverse cast of characters. Mickey thrives on sporadic adventures to exotic cultural locations—mainly because she's a foodie. The only thing she abhors is lima beans. Visit Mickey at: www.mickeybrent.com to check out her quirky travel blog and upcoming author presentations.

JD Burke is a writer, actor, and creative who lives in Southern California. He grew up in Colorado and writes about the uncanny worlds into which he has been invited—or into which he has awkwardly inserted himself. When not writing or performing, he can be found reading so many books he makes incremental progress on almost none of them, or on desert road trips, or sitting in quiet spaces and holding hands with people who feel things deeply. You can find him on twitter at @bustedsuperman or instagram at @thequantumcoach.

Jasz Kuyaté Cabrera is not an author or writer, but a perpetually exhausted queer. They are currently studying costume design at San Diego State University and plan to be a costume designer for pro wrestlers and a self defense teacher for trans women and trans feminine people. You can find them on instagram @jaszkuyate or @SisTrahood. Jasz was raised in San Diego and aims to make the area safer for other trans women and trans femmes by equipping them with the knowledge and skills to dismantle the violence aimed at their community.

Katie Camacho (editor) is a Junior at University of California, Berkeley where she is studying Art and Creative Writing. She delivered the Student Commencement Address in 2019 at Miramar College's graduation ceremony. Katie has interned with San Diego Pride and is published in *Mesa Visions*. She aspires to one day become a professional creative, the kind of artist that gets to do what they love and makes enough to pay their bills. She is from way-too-sunny San Diego, and in her spare time she likes to read, make music, and spend time with her dog and husband.

Joel Castellaw is a theatre artist and educator. This is his first publication. He's a long-time Professor of Communication at Grossmont College in El Cajon, CA, where he's currently serving as the Interim Dean of Arts, Languages, and Communication. Joel created an ensemble performance called *LGBTQ Voices* in 2019, based on narratives gathered from interviews with LGBTQ students, faculty, and staff at Grossmont College. He has worked as a dramaturg at the San Diego Repertory Theatre for their productions of Stephen Karam's *The Humans* and Arron Posner's *JQA*. He has Master of Arts degrees in Theatre Arts and in Speech Communication. His thesis project for his Theatre Arts M.A. was "Out of the Closet: An Adaptation of Vintage Gay Pulp Fiction." Joel grew up in Orange County and has lived in San Diego since 1986. He shares his life with his husband, Marc, their dog Charlie, and their cat Suzi-Q.

Jennifer D. Corley (editor) is a writer, editor, and producer who received her graduate degree from the Royal Central School of Speech and Drama in London, UK. She's the Program Director of So Say We All, a literary arts and education non-profit. She edits the NPR radio series *Incoming* and its latest print anthology, and is the host/ producer of *Listen With The Lights Off*, a podcast commissioned by La Jolla Playhouse. Writings can be found in *Hobart, States of Terror, Black Candies: Gross and Unlikeable, More Monologues for Women, by Women,* and elsewhere. She was a recipient of a Community Voices Fellowship in Playwriting from The Old Globe in San Diego, was selected for Tin House's Summer Workshop for short fiction, and was the national winner of *Lonely Planet*'s travel writing competition.

Leon Dekelbaum lives in San Diego, is forever single, and has worked as an advertising writer for over a decade. In his spare time, he does storytelling on stage and backpacks in mountain ranges, terrifying his Jewish mother. You can read his children's book *There Are Not Monsters Under Your Bed: A Storybook for Skeptical Thinkers* on Amazon, or see his work at copywriterportfolio.com.

Frank DiPalermo studied under scholarship at the Vermont College of Fine Arts where he received his MFA. In 2020, two of his poems were finalists in the Steve Kowit Poetry Prize, a flash hybrid piece appeared in *Ruminate* magazine, and a short story appeared in *Beyond Words* (an anthology of queer fiction). He was the recipient of two fully-funded artist residencies at Brush Creek Foundation for the Arts and Osage Arts Community. He lives in San Diego and hopes one day to own a cat.

Luke Dumas is a writer and nonprofit professional in San Diego, California, and currently serves as Vice Chair of So Say We All's Board of Directors. His essays have been published in *Hobart, Last Exit, Panorama: The Journal of Intelligent Travel,* and others. He is a San Diego native and received his master's degree in creative writing from the University of Edinburgh. In his spare time, Luke enjoys Scottish lochs, reality television, and the trappings of Christmas.

Bradley Dyer was born in Wyandotte, Michigan. He attended Henry Ford College in Dearborn, MI where he accidentally majored in Liberal Arts. He moved to San Diego at the age of twenty-one and learned the hard way that you can't fill a hole in your heart with dick. He is now happily married, continues to write fiction, and is currently working on a book of personal essays, tentatively titled *Sexpectations*. He can be reached at Braddyer91@yahoo.com.

Edward Elliott is the author of several short stories that have won awards in the NEA Big Read writing contest over the years, and hopes to pursue writing as a hobby after high school. This memoir piece is his first published work. When not writing, you can find him watching competitive Minecraft or sitting in trees.

Joe Fejeran (he/him) is a podcaster, writer, and (sometimes) performer. He co-hosts and produces the podcasts *FRIGHT SCHOOL, Art Time of the Month*, and *MFK Ultimate*. In 2020, Joe was a part of *BINGE* (Lobel), a remote performance commissioned by La Jolla Playhouse. Born and raised on the island of Guam, Joe is passionate about issues around inclusion, representation, gender-based violence, the LGBTQIA+ community, and the CHamoru diasporic identity. This is Joe's first published work.

Paul Georgeades is a person. If you like music, you can listen to his radio show at monochromefixation.com.

Raine Grayson is a multi-genre writer who's worked with The Trevor Project and The TMI Project as a storyteller, sharing his story of suicide survival on nationally streamed platforms. His literary nonfiction work can be found featured at *Go Magazine*, The Paragon Press, and Weasel Press. His playwriting has been featured through venues such as The Playwriting Collective, The Tank, NY Madness, KIT Theatre, and The Rosendale Theatre. If you'd like to queer up your timeline, find him on social media @rainerpism.

Brittany "Nate" Henn is an aspiring librarian, LGBTQIA+ educator, and forensic photographer. They spend most of their time reading, drawing, watching anime, gaming and driving their cute VW Bug. They are currently living in Arkansas & missing the California sun. You can chat with them on Instagram @Pixel.Is.Queer or check them out on Goodreads for Queer book recommendations: www.goodreads.com /pixelqueer.

Justin Hudnall (editor) received his BFA in dramatic writing from New York University's Tisch School of the Arts. He has served as the founder and Executive Director of So Say We All, a San Diego-based literary arts and education non-profit organization, since 2009. He produces and hosts the public radio series Incoming on KPBS / NPR featuring the true stories of America's veterans, which he helps craft and edit, and is an editor on the print anthology series of the same name. In a prior career he served with the United Nations in their New York HQ and deployed downrange with UNMIS in Juba, South Sudan as an emergency response officer. He has been showcased by *War, Literature, and the Arts*, *Monologues for Men by Men*, Pinchback Press, and *States of Terror*.

Tyler King is a non-binary poet from Dayton, Ohio. They are the editor of Flail House Press and their work has appeared in *The Louisville Review of Books*, Pandemic Publications, Indolent Books, and other places. You can follow them on Twitter @ Tkingofnothing if you want, but it's mostly drunk rambling about Bruce Springsteen.

Mateo Perez Lara is a queer, brown, non-binary, Latinx poet from California. They received their M.F.A. in Poetry as part of the first cohort to graduate from Randolph College's Creative Writing Program. They are an editor for *Rabid Oak* online literary journal. They have a chapbook, *Glitter Gods*, published with Thirty West Publishing House. Their poems have been published in *EOAGH*, *The Maine Review*, and elsewhere.

Melia Lenkner is an emerging writer based in Pittsburgh, PA. Her work has appeared in *pacificREVIEW*, *Antonym Lit*, and *The Lindenwood Review*, among others, and her poetry was recently re-published in Mass Poetry's newsletter "The Hard Work of Hope." She took up sewing over quarantine, and at this point, it is what's holding her together.

Joan McNamara received her degree in Computer Science from UCSD in 1980. She later graduated from California Western School of Law in 1994. As a retired attorney, Joan is happily pursuing creative opportunities. This is Joan's first publication, unless a law review note published in 1993 counts. Besides exploring writing, Joan enjoys birding, hiking and taking photos in the Anza-Borrego Desert State Park. In 2019, her photo, "Desert Mosaic," won first place in the cell phone category of the Anza-Borrego Desert Photo Contest.

Marcel Monroy is a Los Angeles-based poet, cellist, and queer femme Latinx person with he/him pronouns. His writing is inspired by a blend of personal experiences with addiction, growing up in the repressive and racist American South, and the works of authors such as James Baldwin, Allen Ginsburg, Audre Lorde, and Gloria Anzaldúa. He currently attends the University of California Santa Cruz and is part of an artist collective called Family Dinner located in L.A., where he is working on his first collection of poems and an EP. His work has previously been published in *Mixed Life*, a digital magazine, and will be featured in volume 4 of *Oroboro* online journal.

Catherine Moscatt is a twenty-two-year-old counseling and human services major. Besides poetry, she enjoys playing basketball, listening to loud music, and watching terrible horror movies. Her poetry has been published in several online and print magazines including *Sick Lit*, *Phree Write*, and *Muse: An International Poetry Journal*.

Y.L. Schmeltz is queer, and a lot of other things. After growing sideways surrounded by corn-laden rural expanses, they moved to San Diego, California. Y.L. has been writing ever since she can remember, and is interested in writing as a way to mental health and social justice.

Kelsey Schultz is an alum of Western Washington University and has a Master of Arts in College Student Personnel from BGSU, with a proud career in higher education and student affairs. She lives in Colorado, making people laugh, cry, and feel things as a writer, friend, career coach, and storytelling performer.

Stephanie Westgate (She/Her) is a trans poet from San Diego, CA who recently U-Hauled to Atlanta, GA like the lesbian she is (even though she won't say she's a lesbian, but also that she's not, *not* a lesbian). She is a poetry editor for *Last Exit Lit*, a member of the Lissen... A Queer Slam Community, and an essential worker tired of telling people to wear a damn mask. Her work can be seen in *Ink & Nebula*, *Madwoman Etc.*, and *Cathexis Northwest*, among others.

Joyce Wisdom retired from a long career as a non-profit executive director that included writing many, many, many grant proposals. Her BA in theater served her well after she left the stage, as her career required more and more public speaking. Her life reflects the vibrant, diverse commercial corridors in which she lived and worked throughout her life, first in St. Louis MO, then in Minneapolis MN, and now in Hillcrest, San Diego CA. Both critics and advocates have said humor is one of her many gifts.

Made in the USA
Monee, IL
26 July 2021